Twayne's English Authors Series

EDITOR OF TH

Herbert S

Northeastern University

Coventry Patmore

TEAS 331

Coventry Patmore

COVENTRY PATMORE

By SISTER MARY ANTHONY WEINIG, SHCJ
Rosemont College, Pennsylvania

TWAYNE PUBLISHERS
A DIVISION OF G.K. HALL & CO., BOSTON

Library of Congress Cataloging in Publication Data

Weinig, Mary Anthony.
Coventry Patmore.

(Twayne's English authors series ; TEAS 331)
Bibliography: p. 144–48
Includes index.
1. Patmore, Coventry Kersey Dighton, 1823–1896—
Criticism and interpretation.   I. Title.   II. Series.
PR5144.W4   821′.8   81–2309
ISBN 0-8057-6767-3   AACR2

*To the Society
of the Holy Child Jesus*

Contents

About the Author

Sister Mary Anthony Weinig is a professor of English at Rosemont College in Pennsylvania where she has taught since 1956. A native of New York City, she was educated there by the Sisters of the Holy Child Jesus whom she subsequently joined. After graduating from Rosemont and teaching in Holy Child secondary schools she studied at Fordham University for a master's and doctorate in English. Her M.A. thesis was an edition, with commentary, of some largely unpublished correspondence relating to Coventry Patmore. Her doctoral dissertation was entitled "Diction, Syntax and Rhetoric in T. S. Eliot's Four Quartets." Parts of this have been published in *Criticism* and *Greyfriars*, and its appendix, a concordance to the *Quartets*, is available from University Microfilms. Her critical articles have appeared in the *Massachusetts Review*, the *University of Portland Review*, *CEA Critic*, *Delta Epsilon Sigma Bulletin*, *Romance Notes*, the *Explicator*, the *Lockhaven Review*, *South and West* and others. She has recently become editor of *Source*, a journal dealing with the historical and spiritual heritage of the Society of the Holy Child Jesus, a religious congregation which began its work of education in Victorian England. Sister Mary Anthony has also two collections of poems, *Fire in the Well* and *Rain in the Chimney*, published by South and West in Arkansas. A third collection is in preparation.

Preface

Reawakened interest in the Victorian era extends to its history and politics, its family life and artifacts, its typical representatives and its originals—and among the latter Coventry Patmore can certainly claim a place. What he believed to be his most distinctive contributions as poet in his own day—his interpretation of English metrical law, and his commitment to the theme of marriage as mirroring the relationship of the soul with God—still mark him as highly individual; he is, of course, not alone in claiming validity for a theory of temporal scansion or in championing a renewed theology of marriage. But it is the poetry itself that rewards rediscovery after long neglect, that is fresh and insightful with an economy and a bounty all its own.

This book aims to present a fresh view of a neglected Victorian writer and self-styled prophet. The treatment is chronological, except for an initial overview and the chapter on Patmore's family, and follows the various stages of his literary career, examining the poems as closely as space permits, and drawing on the prose where helpful for a coherent picture of the development of the author.

The first chapter tries to provide the background and flavor of Coventry Patmore's early life, sketching in friendships and literary associations as well as the more surely formative influences of home, education, and extended parental milieu. The poet's interesting and controversial father, Peter George Patmore, lacks a biographer. Some attention to his adventures, his writings, and his circle is essential to situate his more famous son in the context of small journalism, art and theater criticism, and literary hackwork from which Coventry was able to move on to the major quarterlies. Several fascinating sidetracks which in a larger study would yield rich material for a fuller study of our subject have been firmly relegated to the notes. They constitute a sort of unwritten book, and invite the reader to pursue them at leisure, or at least to allow them space.

The main business of the book is a reexamination of a significant body of Victorian poetry which stands on its own merits for precision, clarity, insight, and power. The modern reader can respond to the humor and beauty of the poems without attending to the baggage of Patmore's later prose, or the extravagances of his woman-worship from a position of utter male superiority. Patmore's poems are rooted in immediate experience of life and love and language. His essays and aphorisms have sifted that experience through layers of thought and sometimes through convolutions of argument. The feeling of the poems can be trusted. The prose follows other laws and must be read with at least as much discernment as curiosity.

Generous acknowledgments are due to my sisters and colleagues for their patience and help over the years this task has taken me, as also to my religious superiors and to the administrators of Rosemont College for giving me time and support for research in England; to the American Philosophical Society for a summer grant which launched my work in 1965; to the Connelly Fund for Rosemont faculty grants which have assisted me in the course of my work; to A. F. P. Watts, great-grandson of the poet, and to the descendants of Gurney Eugene Patmore, the poet's brother, for permission to use valuable family material, chiefly correspondence; to the Society of the Holy Child Jesus for permission to use material relating to Patmore's daughter, Sister Mary Christina (Emily Honoria Patmore); to Oxford University Press for permission to quote from Frederick Page's edition of *Poems by Coventry Patmore;* to the kind library staffs at the Bodleian, British Library, University of London, and University of Nottingham abroad, and at Boston College, Princeton University, and Rosemont College at home; to Fordham University for permission to use my M.A. thesis, "Coventry Patmore in the Correspondence of his Contemporaries"; and to Sister Alice Mary Grubb who typed the manuscript originally.

SISTER MARY ANTHONY WEINIG, SHCJ

Rosemont College

Chronology

1874 Leaves Heron's Ghyll for a winter in London.

1875 Moves to the Mansion, Hastings, Sussex. Emily makes vows, teaches at St. Leonards, near Hastings.

1877 *Life of Bryan Walter Procter* written at the request of his widow. *Unknown Eros,* odes 1–21.

1878 *Amelia* privately printed, then published with other poems. *Unknown Eros,* odes 1–46.

1880 Second wife, Mary Patmore, dies.

1881 Marries Harriet Robson, Emily's friend and the younger children's governess.

1882 13 July, Emily Honoria dies of consumption.

1883 Henry Patmore dies; Francis born, the only child of the third marriage.

1884 Henry Patmore's poems published with a memoir by his sister Gertrude.

1885 Begins writing short essays for the *St. James's Gazette* and other journals, continuing intermittently into the mid-nineties.

1889 *Principle in Art* (chiefly *St. James's* essays).

1891 Moves to Lymington, Hants.

1892– Friendship with Alice Meynell.
1895

1893 *Religio Poetae* (a second collection of late essays).

1895 *The Rod, the Root, and the Flower* (brief essays and aphorisms).

1896 Patmore dies on 26 November.

CHAPTER 1

The Setting

I *Background*

COVENTRY Kersey Deighton Patmore (1823–1896) was the grandson of a London jeweler and silversmith, Peter Patmore, who married Clarissa Stevens in 1783. An artist uncle of hers whom family legend erroneously but characteristically glorified as a court painter for Frederick the Great[1] was actually an eighteenth-century mezzotint engraver and copyist, George or Gerhard Böckman, a pupil of Sir Godfrey Kneller. Several Böckman copies of Kneller's portraits of naval heroes are listed among the queen's pictures at Buckingham Palace.[2] Another minor artist in the family was Robert Stevens, Coventry's great-uncle, a naturalist remembered for his botanical drawings[3] as well as for a country home in the Epping Forest where the young Patmores spent part of their childhood. This was in Woodford Green, Essex. The parish register of St. Mary's, Woodford, records Coventry's baptism (11 June 1824), so we may presume that here was the early residence (today a short trip by underground from central London) from which Coventry's mother wrote to ask her husband to bring certain supplies, including "Rabbit and Brandy," which his London landlady was deputed to purchase for her.[4]

Coventry's father, Peter George Patmore (1786–1855),[5] was the only son of Peter and Maria Clarissa Patmore. Preferring a literary career to the family business, he managed to earn a living by writing, reviewing, and editing, partly in the employ of Henry Colburn the publisher and partly on his own. He made his way into *Blackwood's* and other new magazines; he fancied himself an art critic in company with Hazlitt;[6] he cultivated men of letters and wrote about them in his memoirs;[7] he proved himself a good teller of tales[8] as well as a journalistic gossip. He was well read, and he devoted himself to the literary education of his sons, particularly his gifted eldest. Prior to his marriage at thirty-six, P. G. had been something of a man about town and a dandy. He had been involved in a libel suit and in a duel associated with the less reputable side of the journalistic world. Then his strong-minded mother picked out a strong-minded wife for him and persuaded him to settle down as a good husband and father. His bride, Eliza Robertson, was a strict Presbyterian, rather cold and stern, but most dutiful. Coventry greatly respected both parents, but it was the agnostic father whom he remembered with warmth and gratitude. They ended their days in Coventry's home, his mother in 1851 and his father four years later.

Factual information on Coventry's boyhood is not abundant. His brief "autobiography"[9] is really an account of his conversion to the Roman Catholic Church written nearly twenty-five years after the event at the urging of his third wife and of his friend Gerard Manley Hopkins. Patmore speaks of himself as until the age of eleven an agnostic like his father, who "professed to disbelieve in any spiritual existence" but who inculcated in his boys a great love of truth and purity and a reverence illustrated by his rebuking young Coventry for taking "a thick old Bible . . . to sit more conveniently" at the dinner table. The small child's night prayers at his mother's knee were stopped lest the practice "interfere with [his] future freedom of intellect." He records a religious experience which followed a chance opening of "some little devotional book" which led him to think it would be a fine thing if there really were a God he could relate to—then "a torrent of love and joy" filled him. Though only momentary, it "did not leave [him] quite as [he] was before."

As the autobiography continues Coventry brags about his youthful proficiency in mathematics and chemistry—he claims to have carried on original experiments in his own laboratory and to have discovered a "new chloride of Bromine." His father's intentions of sending Coventry to Cambridge were thwarted by "his narrow means," but P. G. certainly did not neglect his son's education. By the time he was fifteen Coventry "had read almost all the standard poetry and much of the best secular prose in our language." He is modest about his "great love and some slight technical knowledge of art," mentioning a prize received from the Royal Society of Arts—his great-grandson Derek Patmore tells us that it was for a copy of a Landseer picture.[10] Another great-grandson's family has an 1837 sketchbook,[11] completed just before Coventry's fourteenth birthday; the drawing is rather impressive, not as original work, but as skillful copying of Hogarth's types (for instance, *The Laughing Audience*), Landseer's animals, and Sir Thomas Lawrence's children, specifically the delicate sketches in his *Cabinet of Gems*, a small book of reproductions presented with commentary by P. G. Patmore that same year.

The only period of formal schooling for Coventry Patmore seems to have been six not very happy months at the Collége de France in St. Germain where the shy sixteen year old acquired some competence in German and fencing but did not mix enough with the other boys to become fluent in French.[12] He spent Sundays at the Paris home of his father's good friend, the novelist Catherine Gore[13] whose apartment in the Place Vendôme was a gathering place for "the best literary and political society."[14] Here Coventry fell in love with his hostess's daughter, a girl of eighteen who, by his own account, snubbed him unmercifully. A long letter from his father at this time alludes to the risks of Prospero's Isle with a real though unresponsive Miranda: "Yes—my dear little boy—but *you* are not a Ferdinand."[15] This "major emotional experience of Patmore's youth"[16] initiated him into a world whose spokesman he soon felt called to be. We shall see in the next chapter the delicacy and realism of Patmore's perceptions with respect to the kinds and effects of love.

But poetry was not yet an overriding concern for Coventry. After the precocious long poems dealing with unhappy lovers, "The River" and "The Woodman's Daughter," which were probably written soon after his return from Paris in 1840, he heeded his father's good advice: "Touching poetry,—if you have any of it in you it will be pretty sure to come out—whether you will or no—but do not entice it out—for of all follies there is none so foolish in its results as the habit of mere *verse* writing."[17] Evidently P. G. Patmore was convinced that his son had it in him by 1844 when Patmore senior got his publisher friend Moxon to print Coventry's first book of poems.

The early 1840s were years of religious questioning for Coventry Patmore. If his autobiography is to be relied upon, he found himself growing into Christian faith from a childhood background of indifference lighted by occasional flashes of theological insight, each of which brought him to a new level of spiritual awareness. A visit in his late teens to his Free Kirk relatives in Edinburgh convinced him that their direction was not for him. A dark season of reaction and reading "in the way of negation"—Strauss's *Life of Jesus* and Blanco White's *Memoirs* are named—did not alter his fundamental intuition, and he turned to Scripture, Butler's *Analogy*, Taylor's *Holy Living*, and Coleridge's *Aids to Reflection*, which last he "got almost by heart."[18]

The autobiography does not mention Patmore's having once contemplated taking orders in the Anglican Church.[19] The omission

implies nothing about the importance of the decision, the seriousness
of the memoir, or the veracity of those who recalled conversations
with Patmore. He simply did not paint that detail into this particular
self-portrait. More than most other writers Patmore seems to have
chosen the setting in which he is to be seen. He exerts something
very like a posthumous control over the material available to Basil
Champneys, his architect friend and official biographer, whose two
volumes published in 1900, four years after Patmore's death, are a
mine for future investigators. Champneys's preface tells us that "Mrs.
Patmore, for many years before her husband's death, had his biography in view. She often asked him about events in his earlier life and
wrote memoranda concerning them from his dictation, copied portions of his letters which seemed to possess biographical interest. . . ."[20] This was undoubtedly helpful, but it did tend to keep
everything the same color. Of the third Mrs. Patmore's assiduity
Champneys writes more privately elsewhere: "She is a literary ano-
maly beyond any previous experience of mine. She cannot write
herself; but, as a critic, shows an extraordinary literary tact; and all
she says is worthy of the closest attention. . . . she constantly gave
me criticisms and hints which were invaluable, and more than justified the very high opinion C. P. had of her literary gifts."[21] She was
his sole literary executrix, although this responsibility had been
tentatively offered to Champneys in 1891[22] and before him to Edmund Gosse in 1884.[23] Gosse's qualifications were eminent as both
friend and critic, and his small study of Patmore is the first full-length
literary analysis, anecdotal and derivative though it is.

At twenty-two Coventry was suddenly thrown on his own re-
sources by his parents' precipitous departure to the Continent after
an unfortunate railroad speculation had left them in a questionable
position. Coventry and his brother Gurney subsisted for nearly a year
and a half on what they could earn by writing for magazines and doing
literary odd jobs. This was an abrupt beginning of a career in journalism for Gurney, and for both boys an entry in earnest into their
father's workaday literary world, no doubt with some help from his
friends and some interest, even on the part of strangers, in the new
poet.

The critical notice, favorable and otherwise, which the *Poems* of
Coventry Patmore attracted helped to bring him to the attention of
Monckton Milnes who later secured for him a post in the library of the
British Museum.

The stabilizing of Patmore's fortunes by regular employment at the British Museum made possible the most important step in his personal and professional life. In September 1847 he married Emily Augusta Andrews, daughter of the Reverend Edward Andrews, Congregational minister at Walworth, whose chapel Ruskin describes in *Praeterita*.[24]

Dr. Andrews, who taught the boy Ruskin and his own children the elements of Greek, had died in 1841, eleven years after his wife succumbed to the consumption which dogged the family. Emily, their fifth daughter and eighth child, born in 1824, had therefore a rather patched up home life interspersed with boarding school as a little girl. She managed her father's household at fifteen, worked as a governess at eighteen, and traveled on the Continent with connections of the Laman Blanchards (old family friends of the Patmores too).[25] She eventually settled with her younger sister Georgiana[26] in the home of her eldest sister, Mrs. Orme, whose "large acquaintance among literary people"[27] included the three sons of Peter George Patmore. Georgiana married George Patmore seven years after Emily married Coventry, and when widowed spent much time helping Emily who was by then far advanced in consumption.

II *A Share of Anxiety*

To the six children of the idealized marriage of Coventry and Emily, life was not as peaceful as the *Angel in the House* prognosticated. Their mother's prolonged illness and her death in 1862 meant lengthy sojourns with friends and relations, changes of school, and eventually getting used to a kind but somewhat prim stepmother. She was Marianne Caroline Byles, known as Mary Patmore, whom Coventry met in Rome and married in 1864.

Milnes, the eldest son (and disobedient little boy of *The Toys*),[28] seems early and late to have caused concern to his parents and never to have got on well with his father. After an unsuccessful start in the Royal Navy he went before the mast, eventually becoming a sea captain and ship owner. He married late in life and died in 1906 at fifty-eight. The glimpses we catch of Milnes in the family letters have their pathos. His mother writes in the winter of 1861–1862 of "cramming tutors' pockets that they may cram Milly's head."[29] The black-whiskered sailor home after a dangerous voyage in 1874, "nearly dying of fever," is now "enjoying . . . dinner parties at great people's

houses" where he "thinks that . . . he really is in his proper element!"[30] Patmore asks F. G. Stephens to invite Milnes to visit—"He
has a great passion for literary and artistic society, & has plenty of
interesting talk in him."[31] But in a harsh letter of March 1890 Coventry complains to Edmund Gosse that Milnes has seriously misrepre-
sented his father

whose great sin against him has been the refusal to sacrifice the interests of his
other children in order to give one of them the means of living like a fine
gentleman. . . . I should gladly have prolonged the silence which I have
preserved, on this subject, for so many years, but that I feel that it will not do
to leave a man like yourself without any answer to charges against me of
unfatherliness, which, if they were true or if they passed for true, would
greatly diminish the efficacy of my life's work.[32]

Milnes himself writes gloomily to a cousin about not hearing from
anyone in his family but his brother Tennyson. "We are the only two
who seem to recollect that my father had a first (or a second) wife."[33]
In the rather grim picture we have of Milnes,[34] we recognize the
lineaments of the irascible father whom he perhaps reacted against
the more strongly for resembling so closely, but as the negative or the
dark shadow. Unfortunately we do not see Milnes's loving and
humorous side which as a Patmore he could hardly have lacked. We
leave him the apparent victim of circumstances which include his
own bitterness and his unfortunate combination of the wrong qualities of both elder and younger son in the parable of the prodigal.

Tennyson, Coventry's second son, although subjected to his share
of ambitious parental prodding, seems to have met expectations or
asserted agreeable independence in a way that kept relations cordial
all around. He became a physician and was medical officer of
Wormwood Scrubbs Convict Prison. Among the many family letters
in the Boston College Patmore collection, several to Tennyson Patmore as a boy contribute richly to our understanding of the context
out of which the domestic and mystical poems—the distinction is far
from hard and fast—were drawn by the artist for whom all experience
and all personal relationships were articulated in "the more serious
and subtle music of life which he had . . . in his heart."[35]

Tennyson at a farm for the summer holidays, or at the Blue Coat
School (Christ's Hospital) where Ruskin had secured him a place,
receives affectionate or anxious notes from Elm Cottage, Hampstead,
or from 14 Percy Street, near the British Museum. The mother's
letters enclose stamps, discuss his allowance (a "Quarter day shil-

ling"), comment on his drawings, suggesting "some animal not copied from a picture, but either from your head, or copied from a live animal." The distraught father urges hard work so as not to disappoint "poor Mama" who "is *sure* not to live very long."[36]

Emily Honoria, third child and oldest daughter, was nine when her mother died. A few years later she wrote her recollections of the last days for her friend Harriet Robson, who entered the household as governess for the younger children during Patmore's second marriage and who became his third wife. The description is pious and full of dreams and symbols.[37]

If the accounts seem histrionic and the demands on the children too exacting, we have to remember that Victorian earnestness expressed itself in somewhat exhortatory terms. There was no lack of simplicity and warmth in Patmore family relationships, but there was need to present a face to the world or to the future. An effort to edify characterized most public utterance—even Patmore's damns were righteous, and his prejudices couched as principle. He could also be, in private and in poetry, clumsily and exquisitely tender, preposterously funny and humorlessly outraged.

Champneys quotes generously from the love letters of the early marriage (these seem to be no longer available) and from the touching letters to his children during Patmore's first widowhood. A great many others to and from the children away at school cover a considerable range of time and offer rich insights into an interesting family as well as revealing additional facets of the complex figure who is always a soloist and sometimes a prima donna, and who both excoriates and depends on the full and varied chorus of his Victorian contemporaries.

III *Commitment to Poetry*

It was during the first period of happy married life, congenial work at the British Museum, and stimulating literary friendships, that Patmore grew to the realization of his peculiar poetic vocation which crystallized toward the period's close in the following diary notations: among the motives for thanksgiving in prayer in 1861 "for my gifts as a poet, and the discovery of a subject on which those gifts can be employed with the prospect of great good to the world and profit and honourable reputation to myself and wife and children";[38] and among objects of petition "That I may be enabled to write my poetry from immediate perception of the truth and delight of love at once divine and human, and that all events may so happen as shall best advance this my chief work and probable means of working out my own salvation."[39] A little later we find the often quoted clue to his preoccupation: "The relation of the soul to Christ *as his betrothed wife* is the key to the feeling with which prayer and love and honour should be offered to Him. In this relation is a mine of undiscovered joy and power."[40]

The idea of the sacramental character of marriage, of nuptial love as a symbol of divine, is the thread which strings into a cohesive sequence all his writing from the early, neglected "Tamerton Church-Tower," through the *Angel in the House*, to the great odes and final essays.

Patmore's associates between 1847 and 1862 included Tennyson; Browning; the Pre-Raphaelites, whom he sincerely admired in an elder-brotherly sort of way; Ruskin, whom he was instrumental in bringing to their defense; and Carlyle, of whom he later wrote: "I was often his companion in his afternoon walks and drives, and spent many a long evening in his chimney corner. I was a good listener, and never thought of contradicting him, any more than I should have thought of contradicting a locomotive at full speed."[41]

The Tennyson friendship had begun in ardent discipleship on Patmore's part, but cooled somewhat as the hero-worshiper became the critic on equal footing.[42] Although Tennyson was fourteen years older than Patmore he married three years later. Emily Tennyson and Emily Patmore were congenial, with the additional bond of babies arriving in alternate years during the 1850s. Supplying "the Bard" (as the Woolner-Patmore correspondence not too sympathetically designated Tennyson some years later)[43] with material for *Idylls of the King* from the British Museum was a family project. In November 1857 Emily Tennyson wrote to Emily Patmore: "I cannot bear to think of Mr. Patmore and yourself toiling away for us. I do hope we may get a copy of Geraint ap Ærbyn, and so stop you. It is the Elegy on Geraint Ally wants, you know. You speak as if there were several Elegies that you are copying. I hope not."[44] At the time of Emily Patmore's death (1862) the two poets were estranged through a series of misunderstandings which, through the good offices of Thomas Woolner, a friend of both, were resolved only nineteen years later.

Browning, though never intimate, was a fairly frequent visitor at the Patmores' little salon and wrote his poem, "The Face," about Emily Augusta Patmore.

The young Pre-Raphaelites seemed pleased to be noticed by Patmore as a poet five years published by 1849.[45] He was consulted by Dante Gabriel Rossetti on translations of Italian poets; John Everett Millais hoped his portrait of Patmore's wife would lead to a commission to paint Mrs. Tennyson's. W. Holman Hunt, Thomas Woolner, and F. G. Stephens remained Patmore's friends long after the Brotherhood dissolved.[46] Patmore valued both the early association with the earnest young artists and those personal relationships that continued, but he disclaimed any conscious adoption or practice on his part of their distinctive theories.[47]

The poetic output of this period is concentrated in the *Angel in the House*, of which Emily Augusta is the acknowledged inspiration. The title is supposed, however, to refer to the spirit of love, not specifically to the wife. Alice Meynell says that Patmore was too steeped in traditions of art to represent an angel in female guise. The heroine, Honoria, is neither direct portraiture nor idealization, but rather a generalization of the qualities—gentleness, compassion, integrity, love—which characterized the poet's wife.

Although the *Angel* was ultimately a popular success, immediate reactions were varied—ridicule for the slightness and apparent banality of its theme, for what, because of the rhythm of its octosyllabic quatrains, George Meredith termed its "dogtrot domesticities";[48] elsewhere a certain vogue based on the superficial prettiness which appealed to many who hailed the author as a sentimentalist after their own hearts (this irritated Patmore more than the mockery hurt); and among a discerning few, genuine appreciation. In most cases the very features which drew hostile criticism were points Patmore had deliberately worked up to what he deemed their essential artistic functions. His choice of meter had followed much experimentation in quest of that form which best suited the buoyancy of the story of happy courtship and marriage. In the narrative proper he intentionally introduced the concrete subtleties, if one may employ such a term, that are apparent to those in love but not to outsiders—her dress blowing against him, etc. Much in these poems must reflect Patmore's own experience. The sequel to the *Angel*, the *Victories of Love*, in which the wife dies, came out in 1863, a year after Emily Augusta's death. There were to have been two or three more sections in the complete *Angel*, but Patmore stopped with this. A new phase of life was beginning.

In 1864 he visited Rome with Aubrey de Vere. His leanings toward Catholicism, which his wife had long deplored and whose results she had dreaded, reached final submission in May of that year. There was no conflict on her account as he felt that in heaven she understood and approved. He always revered her as a saint, and observed the anniversary of her death as a day of prayer and recollection.

IV *Second Marriage*

Mary Anne (or Marianne, spelled both ways) Byles, a convert who had followed Cardinal Manning into the church, was one of Patmore's new Catholic friends. It was not long before he asked her to marry him. He was much embarrassed at discovering that she was not the poor traveling companion of the elderly lady she looked after, but an heiress in her own right. Friends intervened to override his qualms, and the wedding took place in July 1864, two years after the death of his first wife. Mary had formerly intended to become a nun, and continued to live in conformity with a vow of virginity she had made. The nature of her dispensation seems not generally to have been so understood by biographers, but is stated in one account which is probably the most reliable. [49]

Upon their return to England Mary Patmore devoted herself heroically to the six children who had been scattered at schools and friends' homes since the serious turn of their mother's illness. It was only strangers who attributed Mary's extreme reserve to coldness. Although she had little natural bent for housekeeping and society, and the girls found her a bit old-fashioned in her taste in (their) clothes and hair styles, she succeeded in restoring a real home, and gained the respect and affection of all the family.

Her wealth enabled Patmore to give up his museum position when in 1865 he was threatened with lung trouble. They bought "Heron's Ghyll," the Sussex estate he wrote about managing and improving. [50] His new country-gentleman status and the passage of the 1867 Reform Bill brought his antidemocratic political views to the pitch of pessimistic desperation which they maintained for the rest of his life. Patmore, according to Champneys, who had hours of conversation with him to draw upon, "deprecated the shortsighted selfishness which, in his opinion, the enfranchisement of the lower classes was bound to inaugurate." [51] Patmore himself writes in a letter to Gerard Manley Hopkins: "I never could understand 'The People'—indeed, I may say with Sir Thomas Browne, that the People is the only entity which I sincerely hate." [52] In partial explanation we read:

For material improvement, such as the social rise of the working-classes, he cared nothing, seeing that it did not appear to him to involve that spiritual and moral advance which was all he cared for.[53]

It was nobility . . . not justice, that in Patmore's view was the end for which man was created, and the State should be framed to encourage. The object of the law might be justice: the end of the State should be nobility, and since this end or ideal reposes on the self-evident dogma that men are unequal, he argued that institutions should reflect this inequality. To do this they must be hierarchical, that is to say, aristocratic.[54]

Basil Champneys and Osbert Burdett respectively thus try to show the reasonableness of Patmore's position, while he himself in the political odes and later essays (dealt with in subsequent chapters) is most often angry or deliberately preposterous: "I confess, therefore, to a joyful satisfaction in my conviction that a real Democracy, such as ours, in which the voice of every untaught ninny or petty knave is as potential as that of the wisest and most cultivated, is so contrary to nature and order that it is necessarily self-destructive."[55]

Patmore's verbal fireworks and perverse logic probably entertained more readers than they frightened or aroused. His tendency to absolute statements was reinforced by his relative isolation from challenging associates—the brotherhood of struggling writers, his earlier companions of the press, the measured world of the library. For these an admiring family was indeed an acquiescent substitute. The two older boys were mostly away, at sea or at school, and the youngest, Henry, was little more than a baby when the family moved to Sussex. Wife, governess, eleven-year-old Emily who was always closest to her father, and her two little sisters, lame Bertha and lively Gertrude, offered as much devotion as is good for any man or artist.

The risk of turning a study of Patmore into a family saga is a calculated one. His degree of absorption with the multifarious concerns of home and children, which in another household might have been more exclusively the province of the mother, is proportionate to the decrease of his literary output after he became a landed proprietor and no longer had to work for a living. One whole phase of his poetic career was completed by the time he was forty (with the 1863 *Victories of Love*, the fourth section of the *Angel in the House*, in which the fictional wife dies). With all due respect for his lofty ideal of the sacrament of matrimony, it is possible to suggest that he married every seventeen years to keep the home going. He took very seriously his responsibilities as the one stable parent.

V *Abundance of Gifts*

Gertrude, the youngest girl, provides a particularly good focus; letters[56] come from Heron's Ghyll, the Sussex home to which Patmore retired from the British Museum in 1866 during his second marriage, and from London where the family wintered in 1874–1875 prior to the move to Hastings. Emily Honoria writes to Gertrude on 2 October (probably 1872):

We were all very misen after your departure, at least I can answer for Bertha and myself, who retired to our respective chambers to weep. We partially recovered at teatime but the table seemed very empty. Mama was tired with her day at Lewes and went to bed early. So Bertha finished Redgauntlet to us, and we played Whist, she taking Mama's place. We did not like the ending of the story, I never can bear to hear of the failures of Jacobite uprisings. Today has been very rainy. . . . You must write directly and tell us all about the journey, though it need not be a grand composition as the last letter was on the same occasion. I have moved back into my old quarters from which you ejected me and Bertha has been murnahooing over her Exercise, all as in the olden days before the holidays. I have enjoyed the holidays so much, and am so sorry for the departure of my dear little sister and brother. As for you, Miss, you have grown so old that you are more of a companion than Bertha, though you need not tell her so. . . . If you would like, according to our custom, to hear my dreams, I dreamt last night that spiders were eating my nightingales, a dreadful nightmare, as I thought it was by my neglect. I shall expect a letter every day, and I have a right to the first, as I am writing to you so soon. . . . Goodbye for the present, dear Gertrude, with love from Bertha, who shall write to you soon.

(The letter is signed "Emily H. P./E de M"—"E de M" signifing "Enfant de Marie," Emily having been received into the sodality of Children of Mary at school at St. Leonards.) And on 2 December 1874 Coventry reports as an ex-country squire to Gertrude:

. . . We are at last pretty well settled. The new house is very comfortable, but nothing can make up for the pure air and beautiful country at Heron's Ghyll. . . . For three weeks we have breathed . . . a thick, dark mixture of soot and sulphur. As yet we have been very quiet. We have given no parties and been to none. Next Saturday we are going to have a little dinner. Miss Robson is coming, as it is her Birthday, & Mr. & Mrs. Garnett and one or two more. I think Bertha rather likes London. There are a few cockney robins, sparrows and blackbirds in the neighborhood, & with them she is already on feeding terms. She paints as usual, & learns French. . . . We don't see much of Tenny. We offered him to have a room close by, and to live, out of his working time, with us; but he prefers his present way, & we only see him about once a week. . . .

One of Henry's many amusing letters—this one to Gertrude— is from the Mansion, Hastings, where the Patmores lived from 1875 to 1891 in a house that had caught Coventry's imagination on his first honeymoon nearly thirty years before:

Je suis très affligé que M. Maison-de-bois [Mr. Woodhouse, the dentist] a pullé out vos dents avec tant de douleur et de discussion théologicale.

I was very désappointé at your not coming home with me yesterday morning. Papa stayed in London all day, and we were to go home by ourselves, and take the puppy. Mrs. B. and Miss B. met me at Tun[bridge] Wells with a gletcher, navvy and aftman carying [sic] a hamper with my pog [sic] in it. He yelped a good deal on the way home but the train didn't stop at all between there and here, so we soon got home. I've called him "Hector." Do you like it? I don't think "Wolf" suits a St. Bernard. He likes Roy so much and Roy likes him middling. Cat hates him. He don't bite at all scarcely. Runs like jelly. . . .

The domestic menagerie so frequently alluded to in family letters is featured in Gertrude's small book, *Our Pets and Playfellows in Air, Earth and Water*, illustrated by Bertha and published by Bell in 1880. Bertha's animal drawings and watercolors of leaves, lichen, and other such natural objects done with Pre-Raphaelite delicacy and precision might have won her a place in the art world—as an illustrator at least—had circumstances obliged her to overcome her apparent helplessness and contentment with passing her days in ladylike trifling ("the girls go about tea-partying" says "Kate Greenwood on her Grim Visit to the Coventry Patmores"[57] in Lymington, their last home). Ruskin gave Bertha lessons and sent hints: "1. Never reduce Angelico angels to blow trumpets in a letter B. 2. Make your work pleasing to the simple—girl's work should never express anything but what will be as generally intelligible as a daisy. 3. Are there no leaves on the earth but ivy-leaves? . . ."[58] F. G. Stephens secures commissions for her; Woolner advises on exhibiting her work.

Gertrude, the only married daughter, died in 1922. She was in a very real sense a channel of family tradition, especially in its happier aspects. Between the letters she saved and her *Pets and Playfellows* anecdotes we get a fresh view of the adolescent family. The quaint little book, besides reflecting the prosperous Uckfield (Heron's Ghyll) days when the large aviary delighted the second Mrs. Patmore ("my mother" in frequent references), also recalls earlier times at secondhand: "I will end this chapter with a copy of some verses which describe the death and burial of a cat that belonged to my elder brothers and sisters, so long ago that I cannot remember it, if, indeed, I was born at the time," and the verses are noted as "printed before in 'Nursery Rhymes' by Mrs. Motherly [the first Mrs. Patmore], 1859."[59]

Gertrude also wrote the biographical sketch accompanying her younger brother Henry's poems, privately printed in 1884, a year after his death at twenty-three. His father calls Henry's verses "very inadequate indications of the power and delicacy of the mind and heart which produced them" and says, "his spiritual and imaginative insight were far beyond those of any man I ever met."[60] The gentle and humorous "Dicky" distinguished himself academically at St. Cuthbert's College, Ushaw, but poor health and the loss of sight in one eye were hindrances to his preparing for a profession—he had begun reading law before his pulmonary disorders incapacitated him. Champneys quotes many of Henry's whimsical and affectionate letters and immature poems, and E. J. Oliver supplies further material on Henry, Ruskin's godchild, that is not generally available.[61] His death was a very severe blow to Coventry who less than eight months before had suffered the loss of his eldest daughter, Emily Honoria, who had entered the convent in 1873 and died of consumption in 1882 at the age of twenty-nine.

This Emily was probably the greatest single spiritual influence in her father's life, and her vowed virginity as a Sister of the Holy Child Jesus disclosed to him ways of being that his own appreciation of married love had not yet been extended to include. Any reading of the Psyche odes must take this into account. Unfortunately we have no grown-up letters but the few printed in Champneys or in Emily's biography.[62]

At sixteen Emily visited France and Switzerland with Coventry and Mary Patmore and Harriet Robson. Her travel diary shows artistic sensitivity: "Three greys, the water, the hills, the sky; and the moon thrown forward by the distant hills." There are unexpected glimpses of the deep regard and trust that signalized her relationship with her father, and coded passages of obscure meaning and considerable emotional intensity: code—"Josuah,[63] how could anyone love me"—plain—"It is no use talking about being happy when good, how can you be so selfish, if any you love more than yourself be not happy or worse." "I went out a little with Papa and talked of the late event [unspecified] and of M[ama] and Honoria [i.e., Harriet Robson as she was privately called by Emily]."

Capable of strong attachment herself,[64] Emily would have been very sensitive to what affected her friend and confidante, Miss Robson, on whom she conferred the name of the heroine of the *Angel in the House*,[65] and with whom, rather than with her spiritual-minded but somewhat distant stepmother, she spoke about her desire to be a nun. We regret Harriet's delicacy which deprives us of rich insights into Emily's character and spirituality: "When I married I destroyed her letters to me because I thought she would have liked it, as she called me her sister and wrote intimately about her vocation and love of the Sisters at St. Leonards."[66] The whole family seemed genuinely fond of "Obby" as Harriet is nicknamed in many of the letters, and the Robsons of Lewes in Sussex and the Patmores of nearby Uckfield (where Heron's Ghyll was located) were certainly on cordial terms while their daughters were growing up.

A school friend of Tennyson Patmore described a visit to the poet's family in 1872: music in the evenings "from his wife and elder daughter. . . . simple airs," or, at least once, "we played at impromptus in the manner of Lear's nonsense verses. The poet sat reading. After a while someone gave out the word 'Cadiz,' and with a smile he looked over his paper and said":

> There was an old fellow of Cadiz
> Who lived in a place where no shade is;
> So he lighted his cloak, and sat under the smoke,
> That clever old fellow of Cadiz.[67]

The Heron's Ghyll period saw the inception of the first nine odes and the development of the mystical strain in Patmore's writing. He ranged widely among spiritual authors, choosing whatever best supported his convictions. He was fond of employing the word "catholic" with a small *c*, in accordance with which usage he extolled the "catholicity" of Swedenborg,[68] Gibbon, Schopenhauer, and Buddha, although, contradictorily enough, in a "limited" sense! Patmore read theology four hours a day for five months previous to embarking on the *Sponsa Dei*, a work he destroyed in manuscript after some friends, including Gerard Manley Hopkins to whom he showed it, expressed reservations. Its substance is probably preserved in his surviving prose, especially *The Rod, the Root, and the Flower*, and in those odes which were to have been part of the *Marriage of the Blessed Virgin*, the masterpiece he never wrote.

Since this last work was so much of the very fiber of his thought, excerpts from letters during its preparation may be apposite: "I have hit upon *the* finest metre that was ever invented, and on *the* finest mine of wholly unworked material that ever fell to the lot of an English Poet."[69] The following sheds light on his whole poetic approach:

I have been continually engaged in studying and meditating the proposed subject of my next poem. The idea has from time to time, for years past, fixed my imagination; but it has always seemed too great, when really approached, for my powers. I have not as yet the least idea whether I shall ever write a line of it, beyond those two or three "Odes" which are really part of it. . . . I don't at all see at present how the subject is to be treated, but I have the great negative qualification of knowing exactly how it ought not to be treated. And this perhaps is as much knowledge as it is good for a poet to have before the actual commencement of his work. For the discovery of the mode of treating a subject is a great inspiration and delight, and ought to be co-instantaneous with the actual composition.[70]

The *Odes* were by Patmore's own decision the last of his published poetry. His literary work after his second wife died in 1880 was chiefly confined to essays and aphorisms, and eventually to collecting from periodicals (like the *St. James's Gazette* which from 1885 to 1888 had offered him a friendly pulpit) those portions of his critical writings which he thought worthy of preservation. He hoped, partly, to forestall another's less prudent selection after his death. The first group of reprinted articles appeared as *Principle in Art* in 1889. A second volume of essays, *Religio Poetae*, and a book of aphorisms, *The Rod, the Root and the Flower*, were issued in 1893–1895.

VI   Third Marriage

The year after Mary Patmore's death he married Harriet Robson, who had been his daughter Emily's closest friend as well as governess for the younger children. In January 1883 their son, Francis Epiphanius, was born. This last child, "Piffie," was the greatest consolation of his father, who, because of the exigencies of earning a livelihood, had had little time to enjoy the hourly growth of the young childhood of his first family.

The Patmores' personal acquaintance with Lewis Carroll seems to date only from the Hastings years. A tantalizingly brief entry in a note to Gertrude without a heading says, "Lewis Carroll has been here all the afternoon."[71] Lewis Carroll's diary provides a fuller account of what was to him a visit to an eminent man of letters, first on 4 October 1890.[72] Subsequent occasions are recorded with satisfaction; he met Bertha and Gertrude, enjoyed Piffie, "a very bright little creature, who taught me to fold paper pistols," and got the impression that Mrs. Patmore was "a great invalid" confined to a sofa. (Family letters substantiate periods of indisposition, especially once after a miscarriage.)

1891 marked the beginning of a brief but deep friendship with Alice Meynell, whom he considered his finest critic. The kindly Meynells drew Patmore back into a London literary circle where tact and compassion were as evident as wit and good taste. There he met Francis Thompson, whose veneration must have pleased the older poet. A little burst of critical prose—some articles in Wilfrid Meynell's *Merry England* (during 1892–1893) and elsewhere a few reviews of Alice Meynell's and Francis Thompson's work (the former nearly perfect, the latter flawed by "cheap sublimities")[73]—shows Patmore as incisive as ever.

He had hoped to end his days in Hastings where the Patmores had moved in 1875. But a change of ownership in 1891 terminated their lease of the house he loved. Indignant at first, he soon settled contentedly into his last home at Lymington, also on the south coast and in sight of the Isle of Wight. A period of illness in 1894 left Patmore weak, and the cessation of contact with Alice Meynell saddened him. The weariness and gloom of his last year were not unrelieved, and evidence of a weak heart neither surprised nor distressed him. His walks and his conversations continued much as usual until three days before his peaceful death on 26 November 1896.

The man is perhaps best remembered as the Meynell children saw him. Viola's *Memoir* of her mother[74] describes the awed excitement which attended his reception, every visit seeming a momentous occasion. He was kind, though always the autocrat; he spoke much with those he knew well, little, but with an air of authority, with those he did not. He was devoted in his love, intolerant in aversion, and very generally revered by all who understood him as a Christian gentleman and a poet. The following pages will examine his contribution to English letters.

CHAPTER 2

First Poems

"A very interesting young poet has flushed into bloom this season. I send you his 'soul's child'—the contents were handed and bandied about, and Moxon was told by the knowing ones of the literary turf that Patmore was 'safe to win'";[1] "These are a youth's first poems. . . . [They] can afford to be taken with their imperfections, and stand in need of no indulgence";[2] "His ideas are often too great for his expression. But there is good quality in him, that he has ideas— . . . that he does not trust to accidents of rhyme for suggestions."[3] And so on. Private comment, especially that made to the proud father, tended to be enthusiastic. Published reviews were considerably more temperate. (*Blackwood's* tirade is exceptional.)[4] The mature poet's own tacit comment, severe pruning of the early work, ignores much that was genuinely effective on its own terms.

Coventry Patmore's 1844 *Poems*—not too slender a volume, well over a hundred and fifty pages (averaging only three six-line stanzas to a page)—contains chiefly narrative poems with lyrical or descriptive highlights and a few drab spots of speculation or moralizing. The writing is uneven but includes some sustained poems and several passages of real power. The slighter poems are clearly by a young man whose thoughts as well as his fancies have turned to love and to variations in writing about it. In a three-quatrain "Song" the voice is a young lady's pleading, "Dear mother, do not blame me, nor Ronald either, pray!" because they only went for a midnight walk.[5] Another three-quatrain poem, without title (*P*, 21–22), begins "I knew a soft-eyed lady, from a noble foreign land" who died in the fourth line. Then "In the street a man since stopped me: in a noble foreign tongue" he begged and received all the speaker's money; in the third stanza the foreigner's profound gratitude "smote" the undeserving donor "to the heart." Presumably the gift to her fellow countryman was a tribute to the beloved lady. "Geraldine" (*P*, 45–47) summons outdoors in octosyllabic couplets (actually most of the lines have seven syllables) a joyous, laughing young girl, who is however twice asked about "sceptic flittings fine" that "wreathe" her red lips. She too has "soft" eyes and a melodious voice, but the speaker, who sits "sagely calm" on an "old gate" while she races about, seems most impressed by her exuberance. A second untitled poem, "'Tis fine, I vow, to see you, now," reminds a beauty that she will eventually be "Dead to everything but death." Three untitled Petrarchan sonnets are creditable exercises on the return of lost joys, on poetic fame, and on love (the third is quoted below, p. 42).

> My childhood was a vision heavenly wrought;
> Vast joys, of which I sometimes dream, yet fail
> To recollect sufficient to bewail,
> And now forever seek, came then unsought.
> But thoughts denying feeling,—every thought
> Some buried feeling's ghost, a spirit pale,—
> Sprang up, and wordy nothings could prevail
> In juggle with my soul. Since, better taught:
> Truth-seeing contemplation, light that solves
> Doubts without logic, rose in logic's room.
> Then faith came back, and hope, that faith involves;
> And joys—rare stars! which though they not illume
> The clouded night, have glory that dissolves
> And strikes to quick transparence all its gloom.

> Not wholly for the few in whom thou hast
> Trust for strong judgment, work; nor wholly cling
> To gaudy popularity, whose wing
> Was never made for flight. Fame's perfect blast
> Wants undivided breath. Wise they who cast
> For both; wisest who neither serve, but sing
> Verse motive-void as Pythia's muttering;
> For poets are the prophets of the past.
> Rich Spenser, deep-toned Wordsworth, Chaucer green,
> Shakspere, and mighty Milton, sought their fame
> First in their own approval: we have seen
> How the world's followed. Then seek thou the same,
> If, Poet, thou wouldst be what those have been,
> And live for ever in a laurelled name.

Except for a revised version of the first sonnet, "My childhood was a vision heavenly wrought"—which is not a Wordsworthian intimation of immortality but an interesting progression: feeling, "thought denying feeling," contemplation (in an 1853 revision "apprehension") transcending logical thought—the sonnets disappear in subsequent editions; there is no example of the form in Patmore's final collection.

Three substantial poems, "The River," "The Woodman's Daughter," and "Sir Hubert" (later retitled "The Falcon") keep reappearing in later editions and in shortened form. "The Woodman's Daughter" is ultimately reduced to something like selections for an anthology, not without loss to its real freshness and power.

I   "Lilian"

"Lilian," perhaps significantly subtitled "A Poem for 1844," seems at first to have vanished by the 1853 *Tamerton Church-Tower and Other Poems*, but it has been metamorphosed into "The Yew-Berry." Browning in the letter quoted at the beginning of this chapter says "'Lilian' could never be other than a great and—for a man of twenty—wonderful success under any circumstances," and calls the apparent imitation of Tennyson "rather, a choosing Tennyson's 'mode of the lyre.'" It is quite possible that there is more deliberateness about Coventry's whole performance in this highly idiosyncratic and somewhat preposterous poem than is generally noticed. The "Prologue," "The Tale," and the "Epilogue," all in "Locksley Hall" measure, (1) introduce the old-school-friend-narrator, (2) tell, in less detail than thirty-eight pages might reasonably be expected to lay bare, why he became so upset at the sight of a French novel in the listener's room, and (3) apostrophize England as hope of the "giant Future" with most un-Patmorean optimism. One reading the last stanza first would wonder what is being parodied:

> With thy soul's eye see the Present
>   Not alone the Past's cold tomb.
> It is that, but it is also
>   A true chrysalis—all womb.
> Then look forth to the Future!
>   Till that haven's won, be thou
> The great world's rudder always,
>   And, when possible, its prow.
>
> (*P*, 101)

If narrative fourteeners are graceless—parts of the 1844 achievement reminded Edmund Gosse of "riding down a frozen lane in a springless cart"[6]—exhortatory ones are hard put not to be ludicrous. Unless this is Patmore trying to be funny (and there is no good reason to think so), it is Patmore falling flat on his face, a position somewhat understandable when we recall the urgency with which he had to produce more pages to make enough for a whole book and enable his father's project to go forward.[7] "*Lilian* and *Sir Hubert* were written in a great hurry for the publisher."[8]

The premises are simple: French novels are bad; French language is bad; France is bad. No particular conclusion is drawn since all is stated in the preliminary assumptions. This is expostulation with no room for reply. Among French novels "much read in England at this time by men and independent women,"[9] Balzac was flourishing (in the midst of *La Comédie Humaine*, 1829–1850); George Sand was known and imitated; Paul de Kock was popular on a less literary level. There seem to have been both enthusiasm for and outcry against imported fiction; the otherwise urbane Bishop Wiseman expressed misgivings over the prospectus of a new school for girls: "I have some doubts . . . as to the teaching of French, how far, for the middle classes, it may be useful. . . . The present French literature is so wicked that the temptation to read it is better removed, though much indeed is translated."[10]

The poet's own lifelong prejudice against France seems to date from his unhappy half-year in Paris, where the sixteen-year-old Coventry suffered from homesickness, unrequited love, and a lack of communication he did not remedy by mastering the language.

At any rate, a two-fold probability emerges: within the text the narrator is a bit deranged by his unhappy love affair and speaks entirely in character; within Patmore's clear intention he is "doing" a Tennysonian exercise to show he can or to get it out of his system—we are very much in the presence of the disillusioned lover of "Locksley Hall" and eventually of "Maud" (published only in 1855; "Locksley Hall" was in the 1842 two-volume *Poems*), the germ of which, stanzas about a bereaved lover suggesting that the hero is mad as well as sad—"Pass, thou deathlike type of pain, / . . . / 'Tis the blot upon the brain / That *will* show itself without" (ultimately lines 198–201 of part 2)—had appeared in 1837.[11] It might be noticed, but not over-stressed, that Tennyson, too, has an early Lilian, a short fairy mistress poem spoken as by the mocked lover whose extraordinary conclusion is: "Like a rose-leaf I will crush thee, / Fairy Lilian."[12]

Patmore's own comments on Tennyson's "Maud" are strikingly pertinent; both "Maud" and "St. Simeon Stylites" of the 1842 volume

have the serious defect of leaving the mind of the reader in a painful state of confusion as to the limits of the sane and the insane. Both are written with unquestionable power and an undercurrent of "dramatic irony." But it is impossible to discover in either, where the irony is intended to end and the truth to begin. Of one thing, however, we may be sure; and this is, that the vast proportion of what most of Mr. Tennyson's would-be-complimentary critics regard as the expression of his own views and feelings *is* irony. . . . In "Maud" . . . the element of a morbid mind is introduced, less in order that it should illustrate or be illustrated, than as a means of pitching the tone of the work in a key of extraordinarily high poetic sensibility, and at once providing for the expression of thoughts and feelings with the strongest emphasis, and with almost total irresponsibility on the part of the writer.[13]

Although the above may be an eleven years afterthought, it offers a place between bathos and burlesque to situate another sample of the epilogue of "Lilian" whose strident clichés assort so oddly with the normal voice and views of Patmore.

> Mark well the wondrous changes—
>   Mark the ends towards which we climb;
> . . . .
> The wheels are now revolving
>   Which must work all this, and more;
> The hearts of common people
>   Swelling now with precious lore;
> The rustic hasting homeward,
>   To his Paper from the plough;
> And books, that will be henceforth
>   What they never were till now.
>
> The outward eye turns inward,
>   Slowly wedding fact to fact;
> Such harmonized experience
>   Making knowledge, knowledge act.
> While all of this progresses
>   Sense is weakly, vision thick,
> Sin itself has little savour,
>   And the soul of man lies sick.
>
> The creeping thing has dwindled
>   To a grub, that it may fly;
> And those who stand and calmly
>   Watch the present, can descry,
> Upon its corpse-like surface—
>   In its dead, mechanic strife—
> The blind, uneasy motions
>   That precede the higher life.

> The vital warmth, the leaven,
>   The condition of this birth,
> Is hearted here, in England.
>   Therefore, England! Watch thy worth;
> Keep bright the truth that's left thee;
>   Hold suspicious the advance
> Of every foreign spirit,
>   But especially of France.

(*P*, 98–100)

France and French have received more specific attention earlier in the poem. In the prologue the school friend, whom the listener "scarcely knew . . . / On his entering," tries to resume his old manner but is set off at the sight of "a brilliant French romance," one of those "literary panders / Of that mighty brothel, France!" The villain, Lilian's friend just back from France with a supply of incendiary reading matter, had "lips, still most expressive, though deformed with quoting French." Lilian herself was fluent, and before the fall "her lips' mild music could make sweet the clack of France."

The heroine is decidedly sultry for a Patmore girl. "Amelia" (1878) is the most succinctly typed as "Soft, moth-like, sweet."[14] But Lilian

> . . . could see me coming to her with the vision of the hawk;
> Always hastened on to meet me, heavy passion in her walk;
> Low tones to me grew lower, sweetening so her honey talk,
> That it filled up all my hearing, drown'd the voices of the birds. . . .

(*P*, 58)

The story, insofar as there is one, is that Lilian, aged twenty, is corrupted by reading French novels; she rejects Percy, aged eighteen, and transfers her affection to Winton, aged twenty-eight, the importer of the novels. Percy is desolate, but turns to the world outside (France of course excepted) and is cheered by evolution, education of the masses, and other signs of life that Tennyson heroes also notice but are seldom cheered by.

The motifs, especially those showing up in the quotations just given, are like photographic negatives of much in the later Patmore. Compare, for instance, the low forms of life on the rise with similar phyla taking over in the image of the sheep's carcass (which from a little way off seems a breathing mass but is really just crawling with maggots) in "Thoughts on Knowledge, Opinion, and Inequality,"[15] which essay is also a mine of antidemocratic dicta. "Lilian" is about

the only early piece of which this reversal is true. Tentative impres-
sions in most of the others are deepened and reinforced in the mature
work. Whatever temporary purpose of protest or irony this "Poem for
1844" served, Patmore in suppressing it deprives us only of a literary
curiosity.

II   *"Sir Hubert"*

The other hastily written poem, "Sir Hubert," put last in the 1844
volume, was rightly considered good enough to work over. It retells
Boccaccio's story of the rejected and impoverished lover whose lady,
years later when she is a widow, unexpectedly visits him to ask a favor.
Having nothing to serve her, he kills and cooks his one prized
possession, a hunting falcon. After the meal he learns that she has
come to ask him for the bird for her little son who is ill and longs for it.
She is moved by the discovery of his generous sacrifice and they are
reconciled.

In later collections the Patmore poem is called "The Falcon"
(Tennyson also uses this title in his sentimental play on the same
subject in 1879), and has lost its rather abstract prologue about
virtuous love. Severe pruning in the body of the poem and small
verbal alterations throughout reveal much about Patmore's principles
of revision and ultimately about his canons for poetry. A long cut
passage will show both the power and the extravagance of the 1844
version, parts of which were salvaged in the rewriting; the lady has
just come into Hubert's view—in the first version she "issues," later
she "blossoms" from the trees:

> He gave his soul to feasting,
>   And his sense, (which is the soul
> More thoroughly incarnate)
>   Backward standing, to control
> His object, as a painter
>   Views a picture in the whole.
>
> She stood, her eyes cast downwards,
>   And, upon them, dropp'd half-way,
> Lids, sweeter than the bosom
>   Of an unburst lily, lay,
> With black abundant lashes,
>   To keep out the upper day.

> A breath from out her shoulders
>   Made the air cool, and the ground
> Was greener in their shadow;
>   All her dark locks loll'd unbound,
> About them, heavily lifted
>   By the breeze that struggled round.
>
> (*P*, 132)

Patmore's poetic narrative is definitely youthful and exuberant. It is saved from sentimentality by a certain quaintness, and almost alone among the nineteenth-century borrowers of this story from the *Decameron*—Barry Cornwall, Longfellow, and Tennyson also use it—Patmore renders it as sympathetic comedy in the manner of the Italian original. Only Patmore is bold enough to add one mock-romantic touch which allows his hero to be the more human for very foolishness. This remains through all revisions; the final text reads:

> One friend was left, a falcon, famed for beauty, skill, and size,
> Kept from his fortune's ruin, for the sake of its great eyes,
> That seem'd to him like Mabel's.
>
> (*Po*, 17)

III *"The Woodman's Daughter"*

If "The Woodman's Daughter" really was written at age sixteen, it demonstrates a precocity and competence that "Lilian" and "Sir Hubert" do not match. Although in its general outline it is the least original of Patmore's narrative poems—squire's son, forester's daughter, illegitimate baby tragically disposed of—the approach is actually quite fresh. We are introduced retrospectively to "Old Gerald, and his child" who used to spin in the garden "now grown wild." Gerald is dead, his ax rusts, his daughter Maud, "sole tenant" of the old cottage, is crazed. "The neighbours think it strange Maud's grief / Should take so long to heal." Then we hear the real story. The childhood friendship of Merton the "young heir and the cottage girl" came to include his teaching her what he learned from his school books. An apt pupil of "fable, science, history" Maud also soon "acquired the power to see / The second Nature opened through / Deep-thoughted poetry." In other matters she takes the lead. It is Maud who asks "How is it" they "never talk / Of love." It is Merton who turns pale, feels "what he never knew / Till then— embarrassment."

There is marked sensitivity in Patmore's portrayal of the developing relationship, and a fairly mature consciousness of the thin line
between naiveté and brazenness. Maud is a little like Milton's Eve.
The lovers' paradise is intensified for a brief space after two rows of
asterisks. Then shame which "had grown blunt" becomes guilt:
"Maud began to shun / Her father's sight." The patient unreproachful
father thinks of her "as tranquilly / As wise men of the dead." Maud,
having "given o'er / All thoughts of love and Merton," subsides into
two more rows of asterisks after which we see her with her baby
beside the stream, aware that "Her mind is ebbing fast." But her
thoughts run coherently: if she failed to keep the birth secret she
would be scorned and, worse, Merton would discover "The ruin he
had caused." Seeing "The shadow of her little babe, / Deep in the
stream" she has an idea. She feels the water and finds it warm
enough, but recollects that the stream "bears everything away." The
"dull pool some ways off" offers a solution cloaked by two rows of
asterisks. Maud, horrified by her deed, continues to haunt the pool.

Patmore has again produced a successful narrative poem where a
more eminent contemporary's play on a similar theme is weak.
Browning's "Blot in the 'Scutcheon" "was published on 11 February
1843, the day of its presentation at the Drury Lane Theater. . . . The
poem was struck off in twenty-four hours by Moxon, to prevent
Macready from mutilating the play, and copies were ready to be sold
at the theater."[16]

Patmore was "AET. 16" in 1839—a statement affixed to the title of
"The Woodman's Daughter" long after the fact (it is not in the 1844,
1853, or 1878 editions of Patmore's poems); and whether boast or
disclaimer it does imply freedom from whatever "influence" may be
suggested by two heroes named "Merto[u]n" (Patmore's loses this
identification after the 1844 long version) and two heroines who were
"young, . . . had no mother, . . . and . . . fell."[17] Of course the
woodman and his daughter had no escutcheon, and Patmore provides
no death except the infant's, a drowning reminiscent of Margaret's
child's in *Faust*.

The last four stanzas of the final text have a remarkably high voltage
and effective range, condensing as they do three pages of 1844
process-analysis and dropping forever (by 1853) an appallingly bad
original conclusion:

> Maud, with her books, comes day by day,
>   Fantastically clad,

> To read them near the pool; and all
>   Who meet her look so sad,
> That even to herself it is
>   Quite plain that she is mad.

(P, 44)

It is best to forget this and consider the following:

> Merrily now from the small church-tower
>   Clashes a noisy chime;
> The larks climb up thro' the heavenly blue,
>   Carolling as they climb:
> Is it the twisting water-eft
>   That dimples the green slime?
>
> The pool reflects the scarlet West
>   With a hot and guilty glow;
> The East is changing ashy pale;
>   But Maud will never go
> While those great bubbles struggle up
>   From the rotting weeds below.
>
> The light has changed. A little since
>   You scarcely might descry
> The moon, now gleaming sharp and bright,
>   From the small cloud slumbering nigh;
> And one by one, the timid stars
>   Step out into the sky.
>
> The night blackens the pool; but Maud
>   Is constant at her post,
> Sunk in a dread, unnatural sleep
>   Beneath the skiey host
> Of drifting mists, thro' which the moon
>   Is riding like a ghost.

(Po, 27–28)

These lines also illustrate Patmore's practice of tinkering with the diction of "finished" poems. In the second line of the first stanza of the four just quoted, the 1844 verb was "ringeth;" this turned to "cometh" in 1853; "clashes" proved ultimately satisfactory. In the next to last stanza, the fourth line is the same in the 1844 and the final texts, but in 1853 "the small cloud" was changed to temporarily infelicitous "cloudlets," and the sixth line which had read "are coming from the sky" was altered to the present somewhat coy personification.

IV   *"The River" and a "Sonnet"*

"The River," also labeled as written at sixteen, lends itself to a
variorum study, but one wonders why Patmore expended such labor
revising a very young Poe-ful, Coleridge-copying, quasi-gothic romance of the inarticulate lover who drowned himself on the wedding
night of his beloved—who really loved him too but married the
"noble bridegroom" who asked her properly. There is little in "The
River" which Patmore has not done better elsewhere, even in the
early volume, except possibly the peaceful-nature sequence that
brings the poem round through the year as time obscures the harrowing event and the lady settles into domestic *gemütlichkeit*. The
contrast within seven pages is actually less sharp than the following
extreme examples would seem to suggest.

> The weak stars swoon; the jagged moon
>   Is lost in the cloudy air.
> No thought of light! save where the wave
>   Sports with a fitful glare.
> The dumb and dreadful world is full
>   Of darkness and night-mare.
>
> The hall-clocks clang; the watch-dog barks,
>   What are his dreams about?
> Marsh lights leap, and tho' fast asleep
>   The owlets shriek and shout;
> The stars, thro' chasms in utter black,
>   Race like a drunken rout.
>
>   (*Po*, 12)

The lines above describe the wedding night outdoors from the
suicide's point of view. The stanzas below have reached the succeeding summer.

> The sheep-bell tolls the curfew-time;
>   The gnats, a busy rout,
> Fleck the warm air; the distant owl
>   Shouteth a sleepy shout;
> The voiceless bat, more felt than seen,
>   Is flitting round about.
>
> The chafers boom; the white moths rise
>   Like spirits from the ground;

The gray-flies sing their weary tune,
  A distant, dreamlike sound;
And far, far off, in the slumberous eve,
  Bayeth a restless hound.

At this sweet time, the Lady walks
  Beside the gentle stream;
She marks the waters curl along,
  Beneath the sunset gleam,
And in her soul a sorrow moves,
  Like memory of a dream.

She passes on. How still the earth,
  And all the air above!
Here, where of late the scritch-owl shriek'd,
  Whispers the happy dove;
And the river, through the ivied bridge,
  Flows calm as household love.

(Po, 14–15)

Besides displaying virtuosity, these verses can illuminate a study of poetic tone. Comparing the last "dark" stanza with the first "bright," we notice that one stanza rhymes about-shout-rout, the other rout-shout-about. Both have sleepy owls and signal animals. Although clock-clang is harsher than bell-toll, bats should be spookier than stars. Fleck and flit, it is true, are quieter in movement than leap and race, and their context quieter in sound. But moving up and down into the adjacent noiseless areas, we find one "dumb and dreadful" and "full of darkness," the other just dusky and still in both adjective senses of the latter word.

The roll call could continue with dreams, hounds (the "watch-dog" was a "guard-hound" in 1844), shrieks, air. The rhythmical components are interchangeable as rhythmic segments, sometimes even as syntactic units, though with parlor-game effect on the sense if scrambled beyond the point of switching, say, "The weak stars swoon" with "The chafers boom." The very real quantitative difference between these two phrases has not yet been taken into Patmore's formal consideration. Dwelling on this not altogether idle experiment might have saved Patmore from being amusingly called to order by Tennyson for some absolute statements in the *Essay on English Metrical Law* [18] about the natural solemnity of six-syllable iambic and the joyousness of octosyllabics. [19]

Of the other (shorter) poems in the 1844 collection, one that is not usually reprinted is an apprentice "Sonnet" that seems like Coventry playing Dante. It has a promising tautness, but is more interesting for its attitude than for its words. We have here for certain a committed poet, consciously initiating himself into the modes and manners of his great predecessors. A little later Patmore as Felix Vaughan in the *Angel in the House* takes for granted his fellowship with Petrarch. A competence in the idiom of other poets may well be a prerequisite for forging one's own, and assuming a voice and convention with all literary history behind them may be a genuine help to defining one's own position and discovering one's own poetic identity. The Patmore of the 1844 *Poems* has not yet achieved this, but we can already see that he will.

> At nine years old I was Love's willing Page:
> Poets love earlier than other men,
> And would love later, but for the prodigal pen.
> "Oh! wherefore hast thou, Love, ceased now to engage
> Thy servitor, found true in every stage
> Of all the eleven Springs gone by since them?"
> Vain quest!—and I, no more Love's denizen,
> Sought the pure leisure of the Golden Age.
> But lately wandering, from the world apart,
> Chance brought me where, before her quiet nest,
> A village-girl was standing without art.
> My soul sprang up from its lethargic rest,
> The slack veins tightened all across my heart,
> And love once more was aching in my breast.

(P, 104)

V *The Poet Accepted*

That the 1844 poems were taken seriously by other young artists is amply testified by Holman Hunt's reminiscences (where Patmore is included in the Pre-Raphaelites' list of immortals)[20] and William Rossetti's journal of the Pre-Raphaelite Brotherhood. Hunt described Dante Gabriel Rossetti's delight in declaiming poetry, especially that "for which the world then had shown but little appreciation"—Browning's, Sir Henry Taylor's (in Aubrey De Vere's circle which later included Patmore), William Bell Scott's. "Patmore's *Woodman's Daughter* was a novel interest to all of us eager to find new poems." Soon after this, and definitely in 1849, when Patmore's *Woodman's Daughter* had been recited by Rossetti, Woolner expressed regret that it could no longer be obtained at the publishers, whereupon the reciter advised him to write to the author direct, and this led to the making of a valuable new friend for us all, and of [*sic*] an introduction to the most important and interesting literary circle existing.[21]

W. M. Rossetti in a diary entry for 23 September 1849 records the impressive fact that Woolner "was to dine today with Patmore, who had read his poems, and praised them so much [the unpublished Woolner-Patmore correspondence in Princeton University library mitigates this extravagance somewhat] that he won't tell me what he said." Rossetti adds: "This is the first mention of him [Patmore] (as a matter of personal acquaintance) in my journal. I am not now quite sure how Woolner came to know of him, but think it may have been through Mr. Vom [*sic*] Bach, a Russian gentleman who had some employment in the British Museum."[22] Earlier in the diary (May 1849) we read:

We minutely analyzed such defects as there are in Patmore's *River* from Gabriel's recitation. . . . [Millais] having informed us . . . that he had been reading Patmore's *Woodman's Daughter* and *Sir Hubert*, and had found several faults of diction, etc., therein, we proceeded to a most careful dissection, and really the amount of improvable is surprisingly small. . . . [Millais] intends soon to set about his subject from Patmore, Sir Hubert and Mabel, "as she issues from the trees."[23]

William notes, "This was not done." Millais did, however, paint *The Woodman's Daughter* which implicitly shared the *Times* critic's scorn and Ruskin's vindication during the Royal Academy Exhibition of 1851 (*Mariana* and *The Return of the Dove to the Ark* received explicit comment in the *Times* account). Although this painting and Millais's portrait of Patmore's wife, also done in 1851, are cited as evidence of Patmore's inclusion with the avant-garde of his day, the aging and querulous Patmore of 1885[24] writes to another former Pre-Raphaelite, F. G. Stephens:

I remember the Woodman's Daughter picture. It was a charming picture in all save this principal point. The girl looked like a vulgar little slut. The landscape consisted of a wood of tall and slender trees the stems of which, if I recollect rightly, were alone seen. It was very striking and pleasing. The boy was in Millais [*sic*] best manner. Millais painted my wife's portrait for me (a present) but it omitted all the refinement of her face, and had the truth and untruth of a hard photograph. I keep it locked up as I do not like the children to think it like their mother; and for a similar reason I should not like to have it exhibited. [25]

These highly personal sentiments uttered long after the fact (and perhaps colored by disapproval of Millais who had not only abandoned Pre-Raphaelite principles but had married Ruskin's wife) are not reflected in Champneys's plain reporting[26] of the artistic events or in Edmund Gosse's fuller description[27] of the portrait which great-grandson Derek Patmore quotes, adding that the painting "now hangs in the Fitzwilliam Museum, Cambridge."[28]

Patmore's strictures extend also to his own poems. To H. S. Sutton, his Swedenborgian friend, he writes, not long after his first book:

What I meant by my book being damned by a few eccentric and affected phrases is this; that, whereas my verses have now perhaps a couple of hundred readers to whom they may be of service, but for my foolish haste to publish before my taste was matured. . . . I question whether my poems are capable of doing good to any but those who are much better than the writer of them himself. The tone of the "River" is unmanly; that of the "Woodman's Daughter" is of doubtful morality, and portions of "Lilian" are not of doubtful morality at all, but of most decided weakness and sensuality. "Sir Hubert" is alone healthy in its general tone. . . .[29]

We must of course allow for the familiar strain of exaggeration in the two letters just quoted, and in the oracular pronouncement which William Rossetti records early in Patmore's association with the Pre-Raphaelites: "Patmore holds the age of narrative poetry to be passed for ever."[30] (This prompts interesting reflections on the genre of *The Angel in the House*.)

The full story of Patmore's association with the Pre-Raphaelite Brotherhood is too lengthy for inclusion here. It is generally known that it was Patmore who interested Ruskin in defending the new painters. Ruskin's tide-turning letters to the *Times* of May 1851[31] he himself later disparaged as "of no interest or value. . . . I don't think even my father keeps them,"[32] but he continued to write and lecture on behalf of those who before he was aware of them had set out to observe his dictum in *Modern Painters* about "going to nature in all singleness of heart . . . rejecting nothing, selecting nothing, and scorning nothing."[33]

William Rossetti's exceeding deference to Patmore, and Patmore's sometime condescension toward the Brothers—"I was intimate with the Prae-Raphaelites when we were little more than boys together. They were all very simple, pure-minded, ignorant, and confident"[34]—are countered by hints that the poet was also a bore: "Patmore is dreadfully in earnest in his solicitations for me to spend an evening with him [*sic*] I have double share since you are gone," writes Millais in 1854 to Hunt in the Middle East.[35] And Mrs. Patmore was fended off by Hunt before he left for Syria: "I am compelled to hesitate in accepting your proposition respecting the sketch without certain modifications firstly from my own constrained position and again from the difficulty of finding a subject in which Milnes and Tennyson [her small sons] could sit as models."[36] (Hunt's pencil sketch of Tennyson Patmore as a child is reproduced in Derek Patmore's *Portrait of My Family*.)

Among the dicta of Patmore noted by the impressionable William Rossetti is Coventry's complaint or boast that Mrs. Browning "borrowed without acknowledgement"[37] from "The Woodman's Daughter" in "Maude's Spinning," a seven-stanza poem with a moral first printed in *Blackwood's* of October 1846 and included in her *Complete Poetical Works*[38] as "A Year's Spinning"—the resemblance is more in its not very original theme—it is "an imitation (in incident and termination)"—than in biographical details (Mrs. Browning's girl had a mother who cursed her). In general the "influence" would seem to be the reverse. Gosse finds that throughout the 1844 *Poems* young Patmore "is under the spell of certain lyrics published by his elder contemporary, Elizabeth Barrett,"[39] whose 1838 volume had attracted good critical notice.[40] Several of its poems had appeared anonymously in the *New Monthly Magazine*.[41] This as one of Colburn's magazines with which P. G. Patmore was involved would almost certainly have come to the attention of Coventry, who years later was to write an approving, somewhat condescending review-article on "Mrs. Browning's Poems," viz., the fourth, three-volume edition of 1856 plus *Aurora Leigh*. Their value, Patmore opined, "might be, at least, doubled by condensation and a more thoroughly polished diction. . . . Mrs. Browning's worst fault is her almost constant endeavour to be 'striking.'"[42] These and other detailed criticisms by a fellow craftsman and earnest theorist show a rather high consistency with his own practice, noted earlier in this chapter, of revising poems for successive editions. And it is particularly interesting at the midpoint of his *Angel in the House* period to hear Patmore concede that while Mrs. Browning's "highest convictions upon Life and Art have entered" into *Aurora Leigh*, he doubts the place of such convictions in a poem. Much could be made of Coventry's response to *Aurora Leigh* on other grounds: its enthusiastic critical reception shortly

after his "Espousals" (the second part of *The Angel in the House*) had
appeared with no attention from the press, the alleged dig at the
Angel in Mrs. Browning's lines, especially:

> . . . their angelic reach
> Of virtue, chiefly used to sit and darn,
> And fatten household sinners. . . .[43]

A contemporary reviewer, dealing in the same article with Miss
Barrett's two volumes and Coventry's first offerings (both by Moxon
in 1844), as well as Fanny Kemble, Robert Nicoll, and William Thom
of Inverury, awards an easy palm to Elizabeth but warns that although Coventry has published too soon, "not therefore is he to be
thrown aside."[44] He just needed experience and this he was about to
embark upon.

CHAPTER 3

Literary Journalist and Poet Librarian

I The Young Critic

WITH small fame and smaller funds Patmore played a double role of impecunious poet and harassed reviewer. His father's monetary losses had left the sons, hitherto free enough of severe financial strain, to earn a hand-to-mouth livelihood by their literary talents. In 1845 Coventry appeared regularly in *Douglas Jerrold's Shilling Magazine* whose pages P. G.'s name also adorned. Jerrold had won early the kind of success P. G. Patmore, seventeen years his senior, would like to have attained. A reasonably popular dramatist[1] and well-known wit, Jerrold was a drawing card on the staff of *Punch* from its first months in 1841, in which beginnings his serious articles, social and political (and sentimental), signed "Q"[2] were as prominent as his amusing pieces.

Douglas Jerrold's Shilling Magazine, a monthly, flourished between 1845 and 1848 with the help of the same John Leech, "the chief pictorial pillar of *Punch*," whose illustrations Ruskin praised as "the finest definition and natural history of the classes of our society."[3] The short life of the *Shilling Magazine* Kathleen Tillotson explains: "It was probably too radical, and too 'low,' to offer a serious challenge to the half-crown monthlies in that period."[4] Jerrold's "appeal to the hearts of the Masses of England" in a venture supported by the publishers of *Punch* was consistently fostered by both the price and his editorial espousal of the cause of the lower class.[5]

It seems no coincidence that Coventry Patmore's one and only contribution to *Punch* appeared (unsigned) in 1845.[6] "Vive la Guerre! A War Song for the French in Algiers," reprinted with minor but real improvements in the 1853 *Tamerton Church-Tower* as "The Caves of Dahra,"[7] bears out what the author of "Lilian" had in the previous year told us of French manners. It is instructive to compare the two versions of the beginning and end of the second stanza. (Note the maggot image again.)

> Rush the sparks in rapid fountains
> Up abroad into the sky!
> . . . .
> Lo, the flames writhe, rush, and tear!
> And a thousand writhe like maggots
> In among them! Vive la guerre!

(1845)

> Now the sparks, in rapid fountains,
> Rush abroad into the sky;
> . . . .
> Lo, the flames writhe, rush, and tear;
> And a thousand, in among them,
> Writhe like maggots. *Vive la guerre!*

(1853)

Punch[8] like the rest of England was much exercised by the barbarous extermination of a whole tribe of Arabs who took refuge in a series of natural caves, declined to surrender, and were burned to death or suffocated when the French under Colonel Pellissier (whom *Punch* proposed honoring with a faggot in bronze) kindled and lowered fascines and kept the fires going until some "eight hundred men, women, and children . . . perished."[9]

Equally untypical of the later Patmore and as nicely adjusted to Jerrold's social theories is number 1 of "Rhymes for the Times," entitled "The Murderer's Sacrament. A Fact."[10] The more factual and less moralizing portions of this—the opening stanza of section 4 and most of section 2—are included in Patmore's 1853 poems as "A Sketch in the Manner of Hogarth,"[11] with, however, the following note appended: "I understand that these verses, which were first printed some years ago, have been regarded as indirectly advocating the abolition of punishment by death. I had no such intention in composing them." This disclaimer may spring simply from a desire to keep the record straight, or it may be a gesture of dissociation from the Jerrold circle and its crusades. If Patmore was remonstrating against anything in this not ineffective piece, it was public hangings with their brutalizing effect on the spectators. All three versions of his poem retain the following in some form:

> Mothers held up their babes to see,
> Who spread their hands, and crowed for glee;
> . . . .

> A baby strung its doll to a stick;
> A mother praised the pretty trick;
> The children caught and hang'd a cat;
> Two friends walk'd on, in lively chat;
> And two, who had disputed places,
> Went forth to fight, with murderous faces.
>
> (*Po*, 56–57)

In 1845 the babes "screamed for glee" and the savagery of the mob is more strongly depicted. This poem antedates Dickens's *Daily News* articles (1846) and his famous letters to the *Times* after witnessing with a select party the hanging of a Mr. and Mrs. Manning in November 1849. The last public execution in England took place in 1868.[12]

The second, and presumably the last of Patmore's "Rhymes for the Times" in *Jerrold's* is "Young and Old England," a debate in which youthful optimism triumphs. The most interesting thing about it, besides the social and political optimism so soon to vanish, is its reappearance after surgery with the 1853 poems. The date (1846) is added at the end, which is the original end (although the original publication date was 1845). Its title has been changed to "Hope Against Hope"—quite possibly to remove any suggestion of Disraeli's Young England, in full bloom with *Coningsby* and *Sybil* in 1844 and 1845; it is hard to tell at what stage in his career Disraeli became for Patmore the *bête noir* he surely was by 1867. The dully expository first stanza of the *Shilling Magazine* poem has been dropped, and we plunge into the speech of "the youth, with eager forehead, / Flashing eyes, and flowing hair."[13] After three stanzas of the original, we pick up two from, of all places, the epilogue to "Lilian"—"The outward eye . . . wedding fact to fact" and "The creeping thing . . . dwindled to a grub" (quoted above, p. 34). The rest proceeds as in *Jerrold's*, with a few omissions (three of the more pious stanzas) and softenings ("my son" for "young man" or "poor youth," "replied" for "exclaimed").

"Rhymes for the Times" are neither wellsprings of insight nor models of craftsmanship, but plucky experiments of a poet out of pocket. The Hogarth piece is a *tour de force*, a showing of strength in a direction not explored before. "Young and Old England" may be a last heroic effort to do what is expected of a youthful poet, but its vulnerability to scissors and paste is more impressive than any possible earnestness or satiric intent behind it. Either alternative is a less likely explanation than just grinding out verses.

II *Early Prose*

The prose pronouncements of the twenty-one to twenty-two-year-old Patmore run to thirty-eight pages in *Jerrold's* (if everything signed "An Optimist" is his) between January 1845 and July 1846 (the leanest months of Patmore's career), with a few more identified articles in the short-lived *Lowe's Edinburgh Magazine* and the *Daily News*, a new liberal paper then under the kindly editorship of John Forster, perhaps already assisted by Gurney Patmore. Although a little sophomoric, the "Optimist" papers and the book reviews—one, of the *Life of Jean Paul Richter*, even if eked out with substantial quotations, is ambitious enough to be called a review article—show a range of reading, a level of understanding, and a degree of fluency that do credit to P. G.'s tutorials. Excerpts from the "Optimist" offer observations:

If healthiness is the quality of him who speaks from a fixed position, morbidness is the state of him whose position is tottering and unstable . . . who sees old principles falling, and has none to erect in their place. . . . It is an expression of the present age. (I, 491–92)

The poet and the romanticist should beware of furthering the cause of social fallacy. . . . it is best for the poet not to assume too thoroughly the spirit of old chivalry or despotism, or if he does turn ancient minstrel for the nonce, to show that he does it as an artist, not as a man; that he can lay down the lyre as easily as he took it up. . . . All the sphere of nature and history is open to any artist, but let him be cautious as to polemics. (II, 209)

Nature [is] a foe only in that sense in which the marble may be called a foe to the sculptor, when it resists to his force and blunts the edge of his chisel. . . . The sculptor cannot carve an image out of water; the very power which resisteth him is necessary for the existence of his statue. (III, 114)

Patmore is already convinced that the poet speaks for his age as a perceptive and articulate interpreter, not as an inspired oracle. The multitudes who hear him begin to understand what they (the "ignorant vulgar") could neither have discerned nor expressed. The literary man is clearly of the elite. He may lead others, but must be wary of writing propaganda. The learned must not be overly tenacious of their own opinions, but open to new doctrines. English thinkers, for instance, have much to gain from German aestheticians—Patmore's 1845 review of Schiller's letters and essays is generous in praise of

Teutonic metaphysics and loftily disparaging of English "common-sense" and, true to his established prejudice, of French logic with its tendency to skepticism. Artistic integrity demands respect for one's medium and freedom from subservience to utilitarian ends. Poetry humanizes and elevates; the poet is an Emersonian seer.

What aesthetic theory finds expression in these essays is orthodox enough despite its refulgence. The exercises in practical criticism that the reviews represent shine less evenly. The degree of anonymity and agelessness conferred by the general publishing practice of unsigned articles, with or without editorial interpolation, seems to encourage Coventry Patmore's natural tendency to pontificate. "To promulgate sound principles of criticism is one of the most serviceable offices that can be performed to literature." "The duty of the critic . . . may be interpretative as well as judicial."[14] This duty is in any event taken terribly seriously. Leigh Hunt, to whom young Patmore was undoubtedly indebted for helpful introductions and encouragement,[15] and Emerson, whom he admired greatly but did not yet know,[16] are commended like diligent schoolboys. Richter's biography and Schiller's letters prompt reflections on the "fundamental difference in the modes of thought between German and English writers"—in the German and Teutonic mind generally, objects receive their value from the state of the mind itself.[17] Two poets obscurer than Patmore himself (William Thom of Inverury and Miss Eliza Cook) lack "the true element of poetry, that fusion . . . of the intellect, the imagination, and the feeling—an utterance proportionately and intensely mingling all into a new product."[18] Difficult to accept as Patmore's at all is a review of the second volume of *Modern Painters* which confines itself chiefly to objecting to the objections to "progress" of the celebrated Graduate of Oxford, progress being "that word written on our [the *Shilling Magazine*'s] banner."[19]

Through the final half of 1846 Patmore met again the hospitality of the new magazine toward the new writer, contributing possibly ten articles to the ephemeral but respectable *Lowe's Edinburgh Magazine*. This nearly unnoticed neighbor of the powerful *Blackwood's Magazine* and *Edinburgh Review* carried original material like the former and reviews of current books like the latter. Its occasional references to "the taint of Romanism" and "emancipation from the yoke of the Roman Antichrist" make its editorial position clear during the Tractarian heyday, and suggest that Patmore's maternal relatives might be his link with this journalistic outlet. John Lowes, Edinburgh bookseller, appears nowhere on P. G.'s beat.

The *Lowe's* material includes an analytical essay on Emerson, settling upon and discussing with some asperity "the two fundamental principles of Mr. Emerson's philosophy": "I. It attaches no value whatever to *opinion;* but deals exclusively with perceptional or intuitive *knowledge*. . . . II. It regards universal nature as the image, and only adequate expression of universal Truth. . . . in this creed there are expressed half-truths of the most dangerous character."[20] A letter to Sutton two years later (June 1848) expresses much the same concern:

I have seen a good deal of Emerson. He dined here with Tennyson before he went to Paris, and I expect to see much more of him now. He speaks with much affection and consideration of you. . . .
I regret that, admiring Emerson's writings so much, though very partially, I cannot sympathise with him personally. I am so bigoted that I seem to be sensible of a hungry vacuum whenever I do not find views of Christianity in some respects corresponding with my own.[21]

Patmore's Jean Paul Richter reappears in *Lowe's*, and at greater length than in *Jerrold's*. A review of *The New Timon*, generally recognized as Sir Edward Bulwer Lytton's book, speaks out boldly against the "brewery horse trampling among lilies" after quoting from Lytton's attack upon Tennyson—"the criticism of a poet, by a man of strong understanding accustomed to express himself in metre."[22] (This is either integrity or ingratitude on Patmore's part, Lord Lytton having written a long letter, kind and full of advice about reaching the masses, to the young poet whose 1844 volume had interested him.)[23] "Novels by the Countess Hahn Hahn" receive "a broad *damnatur*" from Patmore or his editor—they are "of the true serpent breed, glistening, insinuating, gay, insidious, venomous, and devilish productions."[24]

The articles described above may not seem very original or impressive, but we can claim real significance for one short series of contributions, the "Gallery of Poets" feature, if it is really Patmore's.[25] Considering the paucity of seventeenth-century criticism in the first half of the nineteenth, these essays on Donne, Herbert, and Herrick are almost avant-garde. The editor's note is revealing: "We intend to exhibit, from time to time, such specimens of the less familiar, but worthy English poets, as, along with a few biographical and critical remarks, may introduce many of our readers to a new and engaging literary field, and recall pleasing recollections to those of them who are already familiar with it." There was no separate edition of Donne's poems between 1719 and 1872; Herbert and Herrick fared somewhat better. Restricted interest filtered through individual enthusiasms, notably Coleridge's, and less effectively Lamb's and Leigh Hunt's. These were obvious avenues for the son of P. G. Patmore.

The qualities Patmore points to as most distinctive in Donne, besides "profundity of thought" and the "ruggedest" versification, are his freedom from "false shame" about sex and from personal rancor in his satires. Without actually using Eliot's term, "dissociation of sensibility," Patmore praises another characteristic of Donne and his age, an "instinctive immediate perception" unmarred by "the hyperbole-hating decencies of flat conventionality." George Herbert's "sweetness, accuracy, and elegance" of mind and of poetry remind Patmore of Tennyson, who also "wants force." Patmore commends Herbert's admirable rendering of religious feeling and experience and the unity of his work. Herrick's (few) strong points are spontaneous grace and accuracy in capturing rustic joys and beauties, especially in "Country Life," which, Patmore suggests, Milton imitated in "L'Allegro."[26]

Among modern critics who have noticed an affinity between Patmore and the metaphysicals, Mario Praz arrives at this perception almost as an afterthought to his *Hero in Eclipse in Victorian Fiction*.[27] The book demonstrates that from Coleridge to Macaulay "romanticism turns bourgeois," traces "the decline of the hero" through Dickens, Thackeray, Trollope, and George Eliot, and in an appendix, "The Epic of the Everyday," discusses *The Angel in the House*, at first in terms of the usual allegations with a slight continental twist—the poem is "an incarnation of Victorian Biedermeier." But the appearance in close succession of Claudel's translations of several Patmore odes (in *Nouvelle Revue Française* in 1911) and of Grierson's edition of Donne (1912) focused for Praz a relationship that few had hitherto remarked:[28]

Was [Patmore] attracted to Donne by the theory expounded in *The Extasie* which maintained the necessity and dignity of the sensual part of love ("To our bodies turne wee then, that so Weake men on love reveal'd may looke")? This is likely; but he must also have been attracted by the fact that Donne had been the first to do away with the courtly tradition which banished from Parnassus all common things and common expressions, the first to introduce everyday life into verse, and to find a form of verse which lent itself equally well to the expression of that life and to the rendering of abstract metaphysical thought in terms which the senses could apprehend.

Patmore was soon to break into the better quarterlies, and in 1847 the *North British Review* began to publish his serious critical work, particularly on literature and architecture. He contributed frequently to the *British Quarterly Review* and the *Edinburgh Review* as well as to weeklies like the *Literary Gazette* and the *Saturday Review* during the productive 1850s.

The dozen or so art and architecture articles published between 1847 and 1858 were really reviews. Lord Lindsay's three volumes of *Sketches of the History of Christian Art*, though considered two-thirds dull, are quoted copiously where Patmore's interest is aroused—on Christian mythology of angels, on saints who were apparently insane visionaries, and above all on the need of "re-ascending to the fountainhead" by studying and restoring the frescos, etc., of artists *before* Raphael. [29] We begin to see how young Patmore came to be an "authority" to the younger Pre-Raphaelites a few years later. This somewhat superficial piece in a March 1847 *Critic* (a weekly) was followed in two May numbers by parts 1 and 2 of a rather pretentious review of Schelling's *Philosophy of Art*. Patmore had dipped into this sea of thought before, in the *Shilling Magazine* Schiller article referred to above (p. 50). One issue is the imitation of nature—art should "surpass her actual realizations." Such a view was all right with Patmore, who had reservations, however, about Schelling's position (which Carlyle and Emerson favored) on the "unconscious energy [which] must unite itself" to the conscious activity of the artist. Patmore wanted to be no "passive instrument of nature" but "her voluntary interpreter and priest"—more godlike, less pantheistic. [30]

"The Aesthetics of Gothic Architecture" is a thirty-page *British Quarterly Review* article spinning off from four books including a translation of a fifteenth-century treatise on church symbolism and Ruskin's *Seven Lamps of Architecture*. Patmore in a knowing way cites authorities beyond his immediate authors, whose mistakes he points out, offering, for instance, a few more "lamps" than Ruskin had proposed. [31] Patmore had already crossed swords with Ruskin, whom he thought too worshipful of Nature, in an 1846 *Shilling Magazine* review of *Modern Painters*, volume 2. [32]

"Ethics of Art," also in the *British Quarterly Review* (1849), is an article Patmore himself wanted to preserve. It makes a little clearer his leaning toward an Aristotelian "imitation" of what ought to be. The five books it is meant to review are Coleridge's *Lectures on Shakespeare*, von Schlegel's *Aesthetic and Miscellaneous Works*, some new *Lives of the Italian Painters, An Inquiry into the Philosophy and Religion of Shakespeare,* and the *Life and Pontificate of Leo X,* a patron of the arts.[33] The touch of pomposity in Patmore's remarks may reflect standard reviewing style as well as the example of his skillful father.

Two more long articles, mostly on Ruskin, appeared in the *North British Review* in 1850–1851.[34] Dealing with the *Seven Lamps* again and with the first volume of the new *Stones of Venice,* and referring to the recent "Aesthetics of Gothic" (*British Quarterly Review*), these seem in Patmore's mind to constitute a series, as much a history of architecture as an exposition of Ruskin's teaching which he quotes and praises. Patmore's basic recommendation of Ruskin's "bold and genial discourse" is heard yet again in *British Quarterly Review* in 1851 (*Stones*) and in the *Edinburgh Review* of the same year (*Lamps* and *Stones*).[35]

As review articles dealing with much the same material, these essays are understandably repetitious. Ideas and opinions which Patmore continued to hold found their way into his later work (see pp. 112–23). Early and late he had something to say about selectivity. In 1847 he wrote to his friend H. S. Sutton:

I don't agree with you as to the *transitory* good of talking. In fact, I question whether it would not be better for those who really can think, to abstain entirely from the time-wasting process of writing. . . . I am certain that my views of art, for instance, can never be lost, if I never put them on paper. I have told them to two or three, and the seed is sown! . . . Let me warn you, my dear friend, against judging of me by what I write to you just now. I am at present in my matter of fact phase of existence, or rather of endeavour and thought. Therefore you must receive all that I say with a certain degree of caution. I have passed through several phases. Three years ago I was in the Emersonian phase: one year ago I was in the Calvinistic Faith-versus-Work phase, and so on. I have not a many-sided mind: I can only do one thing at the [*sic*] time. I shall strive, under your tuition, to enter upon the Love phase; for Love, like Belief and everything else, seems to be a matter, not perhaps of the *will*, but certainly of *choice*.[36]

We can take seriously if not too literally an 1886 statement of Patmore in a letter to Harry Buxton Forman:

Between 1846 and 1862 I wrote a great many articles in the Edinburgh, North British, and National (Quarterly) Review, and in other periodicals; but the only Papers I desire to have my name connected with are, an article "on the Sources of Expression in Architecture" in the Edinburgh [this review of

Ruskin's *Seven Lamps of Architecture* and *Stones of Venice* is absorbed into
the essay "Architectural Styles" in *Principle in Art*]; "English Metrical Critics" in the North British [reprinted with the 1878 collected poems] . . . ; a
paper on the "Ethics of Art" [*British Quarterly Review*, 1849] . . . ; an Article
on "Shakespeare," beginning "The Drama of Shakespeare was an invention
of his own" [*North British Review*, 1849].[37]

III   *British Museum, Milnes, Keats*

Patmore worked at the British Museum for nearly twenty years,
from his appointment in 1846 as "one of the supernumerary Assistants
in the Department of Printed Books"[38] until he became a landed
proprietor in Sussex with the purchase of Heron's Ghyll in 1866. He
enjoyed meeting distinguished visitors, such as Emerson (1848). He
was much involved in the preparation of the general catalog of printed
books only then becoming accessible to the public. As a veteran staff
member he wrote an informative and quite professional-sounding
article on "The Library of the British Museum,"[39] full of insights,
information on acquisition policy, comparative statistics, and even
technical observations on such matters as pasting in slips for new
entries in the large bound catalog volumes.

From this vantage point too Patmore assisted his benefactor,
Monckton Milnes, in the initial preparation of his *Life and Letters of
Keats* (1848) and continued to supply data helpful for the editions of
1863 and 1867. One of Patmore's services was the identification of
unsigned critical articles. Of some thought to be by Hazlitt until an
unnamed authority pronounced otherwise, Patmore declared on
internal evidence:

If they are not [Hazlitt's], they can have been written by no one else than my
Father. When I first read them, I attributed them at once to my father, who
wrote in the London Magazine, and also wrote some important eulogistic
articles on Keats,—I was never informed where. The articles are full of his
favourite quotations from Shakespeare, etc., and are exactly in his early style,
which was exactly like Hazlitt's—only I thought, on further consideration at
the time, that the boldness and decision of the views pointed them out as
rather belonging to Hazlitt.[40]

Patmore also tracked down pieces of Keats's own periodical prose,
stage criticism in the *Champion*, also after the manner of Hazlitt.[41]

Patmore was not really a collaborator—Milnes does not give him
credit in his acknowledgments—but copied many of Keats's letters

(not too accurately according to Keats's more recent editor, Rollins).[42] On 23 February 1847, Patmore wrote: "The volume of Keats's letters reached me last night in safety. It will indeed, as you say, be a labour of love to me to transcribe them."[43] The fascination Keats held for Patmore comes through strongly in a letter to Milnes a month later accompanying the finished assignment:

> This [*sic*] interest of these last letters, with Severn's, is nothing short of *frightful* to me. I leave off copying them, with much the same impression as I awoke with, last night, after a very dreadful nightmare. Seldom has there appeared a contribution to some future "Philosophy of Human Nature" of such importance as your "Life of Keats" will be.
> With many thanks for the favour of having been among the first to see all these terrible letters—for, from the beginning there was a whisper of the end. . . .[44]

Either the ambivalence of Patmore's response to Keats or the chameleon quality of his response to his friends shows in two other letters of this time. A postscript of 26 February 1847 to H. S. Sutton (who seems generally to evoke smugness or righteousness in Patmore) reads like a proclamation:

> Upon casting my eye over your letter, I see you ask me what I think of John Keats. I am now about to shock you again! Keats one day read his "Ode to Pan" in "Endymion" to Wordsworth, and asked him what he thought of it. "It is a pretty piece of Paganism," replied the Christian Poet. Keats's poems collectively are, I should say, a very *splendid* piece of paganism. I have a volume of Keats's manuscript letters by me. They do not increase my attachment to him. But his power of expression is truly wonderful. To him
>
> "'Life, like a dome of many-colored glass,
> Stained [*sic*] the white radiance of Eternity.'
>
> May it not do so to you and me."[45]

(Patmore is obviously quoting from memory, but it is not clear whether he thinks he is quoting Keats or knows he is quoting Shelley's *Adonais*.) Alfred Fryer, another friend of Sutton, writes to him (17 March 1847) of a visit from Patmore who "talked splendidly to us for four hours. We think more highly of him from his conversation than even from his poems. . . .Coventry says that 'if Keats had lived ten years longer he would have been the greatest man we ever had'

. . . he says Keats's letters are equal to the writings of Emerson, and resemble them."[46]

As if in reluctance to submit to the older man's influence, or perhaps as an implicit denial of subservience to Milnes, Patmore's review of the *Life and Letters of Keats* concludes a bit loftily with: "Mr. Milnes will pardon us if our deductions from the data with which he has supplied us, do not wholly coincide with his own inferences." Milnes claimed full genius where Patmore saw only promise in Keats.[47]

Milnes, incidentally, continued to be Patmore's benefactor: he is thanked for "the Card for Lord Northampton's Soirées" and for a fifteen pound loan (toward marrying, Derek Patmore suggests);[48] he and Mrs. Procter stand godparents for the first son, and he secures his namesake a place as a naval cadet.[49] Coventry dedicates *Tamerton Church-Tower* to him and sends him autograph letters from the late P. G.'s collection.[50] As Lord Houghton (Milnes was given a baronetcy in 1863) he is expected to be aware of ten-year-old motherless Emily staying with Mrs. Marshall, daughter of Lord and Lady Monteagle and cousin of Aubrey De Vere (how Patmore relished aristocratic connections!)—"Lord Houghton's little girls are very nice, and you will like them very much I think. You do not tell me what Lord Houghton said to you. . . ."[51] In 1876 Patmore, now of the landed gentry, asks Lord Houghton for an appointment to the East Sussex Commission of the Peace.[52] The closest Coventry got to the "Mephistophelean" and "corrupt" Milnes of Swinburne legend and the celebrated Fryston library of erotica seems to have been a bachelor breakfast party at Milnes's London residence in June 1861, at which his fellow guests included Aubrey De Vere, Swinburne, and Richard Burton.[53]

How much of Patmore's concern with Keats was prompted by his work for Milnes's *Life and Letters*, and how much was the faintly jealous discovery of a poet by a poet with a different approach to the same domain, it would be hazardous to guess. Years later Patmore's discomfort with Keats was to crystallize in his reaction to the letters of Keats to Fanny Brawne. Harry Buxton Forman's edition of these in 1878 had caused rather general consternation: they were "vulgar"; it was unmanly to "howl and snivel" so (says Swinburne!).[54] Patmore's pronouncement to Forman (ten years later?—Rollins, Champneys, and Forman's son accept the date) appears in Champneys and is cited in Maurice Buxton Forman's 1935 preface to Keats's letters. It is altogether possible that Champneys has excised portions, since at least one phrase, "wonder and bedazement," quoted by Forman is not found in Champneys, who is known to have deleted elsewhere without indicating omissions. In a letter to Forman of 15 November 1888, Patmore writes:

> I have read your book of Keats's letters to Fanny Brawne, and I think that you may like to know what is my impression of them, though it may differ widely from your own. They are very interesting to me as confirming . . . that Keats was incapable of real passion, and personally not only feminine (which is a beautiful characteristic, even in a man) but effeminate and sensual rather than sensuous (in the Miltonic sense;—"simple, sensuous and passionate"). True passion seems to me to be the energy of the whole being—intellectual, voluntary, effectual, and "sensuous"; but I find nothing in these letters that deserves a better name than "lust," which, when compared with the integrity of heat in true passion is toad-cold. I fancy I detect artifice and cold self-consciousness in his most rhapsodical out-pourings. [55]

Even when Patmore tries to give a balanced view of Keats his distaste shows through. *Principle in Art*, a collection of Patmore's *St. James's Gazette* essays of the late 1880s, includes his review-article on Sidney Colvin's first small book on Keats. [56] (Colvin's full study was still thirty years off.) Patmore praises the critic's temperateness: "The bulk of Keats's poetry, including 'Endymion,' is estimated at its true worth, which as Keats—the severest judge of his own work—knew and confessed, was not much." At the same time, however, Patmore calls "La Belle Dame Sans Merci" "probably the very finest lyric in the English language." [57] Patmore's essay on Keats carries his own characteristic thinking into the body of his poetic theory, bringing to bear his categorization of masculine and feminine qualities (intellect versus sensitivity, etc.), and indeed "when the analogy purports to be more than a metaphor, it leads Patmore into errors of judgment, as it does in his analysis of Keats." [58]

But this is anticipating the heyday of the crotchety sage. Patmore has still a long way to go before he can afford to indulge his critical fancy in a form to impose on posterity. He has first to earn a living, raise a family, and solidify his poetic fame.

CHAPTER 4

Established Poet

I Tamerton Church-Tower

A significant step on Coventry Patmore's way from new poet to household poet (a tenuous position at best, but justified in the 1860s by the large British and overseas sales of the *Angel*) is "Tamerton Church-Tower," title poem of the 1853 collection.[1] This in its final form is a carefully crafted piece whose four parts of different lengths but subtle symmetry are a regrouping, a hundred lines reduced, of the original ten sections. It is tempting, though not profitable, to see in the four-fold division an analogy with the four finished parts of the *Angel in the House*, which likewise moves through courtship, wedded bliss, bereavement, peace (though not with the same couple). One hundred and fifty-five quatrains (in the Oxford edition no longer typographically distinct as in 1853) are not yet the octosyllabics of the *Angel* but frank fourteeners (divided eight and six) carrying with elasticity of mood and tempo and easy rhymes the muted narrative and pleasingly understated symbolism. The phrasing is cut to the order of the four-beat/three-beat sequence with very little enjambement and word order somewhat stilted for the modern ear. But once past the barrier of hyperregularity and spelled out (or rather unspelled) elisions, the reader who gives himself to imagery and language will enjoy the remarkable economy of means, acuteness of observation, and precision of diction which Patmore's good journeyman's hand turned out with enviable proficiency. Recognize, for example, the coming storm:

> The heavy sign-board swung and shrieked,
>   In dark air whirl'd the vane,
> Blinds flapped, dust rose, and, straining, creak'd
>   The shaken window-pane;

> And, just o'erhead, a huge cloud flung,
>> For earnest of its stores,
> A few calm drops, that struck among
>> The light-leaved sycamores.

> > > > > > (*Po*, 35)

This passage is an example of Patmore's more felicitous revision. The drops on the sycamores were originally and less plausibly in a quatrain right after the "long-forgotten breeze" had begun to "move [later changed to "stir"] the higher trees" and before the travelers reached the town and its inn where the coming-storm motif is stengthened in terms of concrete experience of weather, and the description is thoroughly realistic.

The story is deceptively simple. Two friends, Frank and the first-person narrator, who are opposite character types, as practical man versus dreamer, make a day's journey on horseback from Tamerton in Cornwall down to the south coast where the protagonist's unspecified and "unseen kin . . . did [their] coming bide." On the way they talk of Frank's fiancée, Bertha, and of the beautiful Blanche whom the protagonist is longing to meet and effectively falls in love with as he thinks about her, until "The hills between us were become / A weight upon my heart" (*Po*, 35). The trip down takes the two hundred and forty lines of part 1. In part 2, only slightly pruned from the original version, a courtship and double wedding are dispatched within twenty-eight lines. Part 3 (156 lines) renders with significant detail the summer afternoon's boating of the two young couples and the sudden squall in which Blanche is drowned. Part 4 (196 lines) is the return journey of the bereaved, alone and a year later, "from Edgecumb to the North." Patmore's artistry here is cunning, and in the main successful.

Frank's fading from the story reinforces our feeling that in part 1 he is not so much foil to the first-person narrator as his complementary alter ego. Frank has a real fiancée; the "I" dreams of one. Frank is unsentimental, teasing, interrupting with a joke the other's solemn moralizing, "like / The Fool in an old Play." Frank sings a tipsy song, but "I rode in silence." Frank like a hard-bitten prophet warns of the coming storm in the south; "'Behold,' I cried, 'the storm comes not; / The northern heavens grow fair.'" As they weary, Frank says "'Tis wicked to be weak" to the other's "We faint, within the heart." Also, "'I dream,' yawn'd Frank, 'and wake to find / My Goddess a green goose!'" caps the other's longer-winded musing-supposing speech about love deceived or inadequate.

By the return journey the protagonist has grown into a more integrated person through his manly grief. During the deliriously happy interval of wedded life

> I could not toil; I seldom pray'd:
>   What was to do or ask?
> Love's purple glory round me play'd,
>   Unfed by prayer or task.
>
>   (*Po*, 41)

But after his great sorrow

> . . . sweet was the relief of light
>   Within my restless eyes;
> For then I rose to prayer and toil,
>   Forgat the ocean's moan,
> Or faced the dizzy crash and coil
>   That drown'd its mournfuller tone.
>
>   (*Po*, 47)

The clouds, birds, insects, and abstractions of the trip down are supplemented on the return by signs and representatives of human industry and vitality: peat-cutters, a railroad, the churchbells at Tavistock plus its vicar "wide as Asia and as weak"[2] and his lovely daughter Ruth—"in the maiden path she trod / Fair was the wife foreshown"—with whom we might expect some follow-up, the shouting children, lively flocks, and hymn-singing "alms-taught scholar . . . on her happy way." The languid sky and imaginatively described cloud shapes ("magic woman," "prophet wild") at various points on the way down are replaced by a western breeze and a rainbow. The vane that the "dark air whirl'd" in Tavistock the first time through is later "the golden weather-cock, / . . . whelm'd in happy light" or "the gilt vane" that "reel'd / And pois'd." On the down trip gloomy Dartmoor threatened sunny Tavistock; next time "sunny Dartmoor seem'd to mock / The gloom," and the rain of the early morning stopped at Tavistock. The protagonist's restless yearning during the first pause at the bridge yields to "deep and sober joys / From the heart-enlarging hills" as, on the return, he "sat, until the first white star / Appear'd." At this point, indeed, with a righteousness that would be implausible except that it *is* characteristic of youth, he commends peace to the reader too who realizes: "God proffers all, 'twere grievous sin / To live content in less!" (*Po*, 52). We are reassured when the last stanza admits that "My sight, once more, was dim for her / Who slept beneath the sea" (*Po*, 53), as he speeds to the friends and kin of whom he had "mused with joy" at the halfway mark because they "did [his] coming bide," presumably with deeper feelings than he could have attributed to his "unseen" southern kin of whom the same phrase is used on the way down. But in 1853 the stanza opened: "My sight grew moist. 'Twas not for her / Who slept beneath the sea."

This revision of first intention is understandable in the light of Patmore's own bereavement within ten years after *Tamerton Church-Tower* was published, and it confirms the reader's sense of a certain ambivalence throughout. The headlong romance and instant uxoriousness are mildly but more explicitly censured in the original. The vicar of Tavistock murmurs early and late:

> Christ speed and keep thee still
> From frantic passions, for they die
> And leave a frantic will.
>
> (*Po*, 50)

His longer speech in 1853 had included these stanzas:

> Best fruits come not of sunniest years;
>   Good use have griefs; they try
> The sacred faculty of tears,
>   And man with man ally.
>
> Misfortunes show us sins concealed,
>   As slugs come out in rain;
> And the heart's wants are all reveal'd
>   Unto the heart in pain.
>
> (*T*, 46)

The "sins conceal'd" are no more specific than the general romantic debility alluded to early in the first journey: "My life, 'twas like a land of dreams, / Where nothing noble throve" (*Po*, 33). The protagonist's wooing may have been precipitate but his sensuality was gentle and within the proprieties. Hints of the courtly are caught in the blazon of Blanche's beauties with which Frank tempts his friend and in the

Arthurian tales recalled as they watch the sunset over distant Tin-
tagel. Frank the storyteller "told how Merlin there . . . beguiled"
Duke Gorloy's wife, contriving the birth of "Uther's princely child"
and

> How Pelles, loving fair Ettarde,
>   Forgat himself and God;
> And how, by sorrow stricken hard,
>   He woke and bless'd the rod.

(T, 37)

The Arthurian quatrains are dropped after 1853, a single reference
remaining (to Pelles again) in Frank's song during the tragic boatride.
Other omissions reduce the moralizing and make a little bit truer
Edmund Gosse's description of "Tamerton Church-Tower" as

an experiment of the same class as so many which we have since been made
accustomed to by the writers who call themselves "symbolists" or "impres-
sionists." It bears the appearance, which may, however, be illusory, of having
been thrown off with extreme rapidity, and subjected to no revision, by a
bard desirous of producing an absolutely fresh impression.[3]

But Patmore set himself a difficult task in this poem. His mingled
sympathy and disapproval have only the voice of the immature lover
with which to speak. There are not here the extranarrative passages
which as "preludes" to each canto of the *Angel* drain off reflective
matter and allow the hero (it begins to be possible to designate the
Angel's first person narrator as hero)[4] to get on with his delicate
emotions. Two courses are open to the reader. He can search for
missed clues and notice that the journey down and the journey up
suggest indulgence and restraint in the way the speaker manages his
feelings, that Frank the man of action always wants to be up and going
when the storm seems about to overtake them but his overwrought
friend would let himself be swept away while denying the danger—
we hardly need the old morality allusion to remind us that storms
stand for passions. Or the reader can situate the final form of "Tamerton Church Tower" in the context of Patmore's corpus, immediately
preceding and implicitly corrected by book 1 of the *Angel in the
House* where the circumspect Felix behaves so well.

That Patmore has other ways of suggesting the tenuousness of first
love "Lilian" and its later substitute, "The Yew-berry," remind us—
their theme is weak woman alienated by faithless friend. The lady of

"The River" marries another but is blameless because the "lowly youth," her lover, never spoke up. Interestingly enough, as the latter drowns himself on the wedding night,

> "Wake, wake, oh wake!" the Bridegroom now
>   Calls to his sleeping Bride:
> "Alas, I saw thee, pale and dead,
>   Roll down a frightful tide!"

(*Po*, 13)

The love-and-death motif is dominant in *Tamerton Church-Tower* where it is actually the central thread. But Patmore did not limit his preoccupation with the love-death link to plot lines where it was integral. Even the happy Felix of "The Espousals" (book 2 of the *Angel in the House*) "rehearsed the losing of a wife" on the eve of his own marriage, imagining the sequel such as "At morn remembering by degrees / That she I dream'd about was dead" (*Po*, 178) and thoroughly frightening himself:

> "What," I exclaimed, with chill alarm,
>   "If this fantastic horror shows
> "The feature of an actual harm!"
>   And, coming straight to Sarum Close,
> As one who dreams his wife is dead,
>   And cannot in his slumber weep,
> And moans upon his wretched bed,
>   And wakes, and finds her there asleep,
> And laughs and sighs, so I, not less
>   Relieved, beheld, with blissful start,
> The light and happy loveliness
>   Which lay so heavy on my heart.

(*Po*, 179)

This poignantly anticipates one of the real bereavement odes, "The Azalea" (one hesitates to say that Patmore borrowed from an earlier fiction to image his experience here; Champneys quotes from an actual diary entry for 23 August 1862: "Last night I dreamed that she was dying: woke with unspeakable relief to find that it was a dream; but, a moment after, to remember she was dead"):[5]

At dawn I dream'd, O God, that she was dead,
And groan'd aloud upon my wretched bed,
And waked, ah, God, and did not waken her,

But lay, with eyes still closed,
Perfectly bless'd in the delicious sphere
By which I knew so well that she was near,
My heart to speechless thankfulness composed.
Till 'gan to stir
A dizzy somewhat in my troubled head—
It *was* the azalea's breath, and she *was* dead!

(*Po*, 362)

Convention, bent of mind, or premonition, the death of a wife seems a familiar thought to Patmore.

One more point that teases in "Tamerton Church-Tower" is the presentation of Ruth, "a girl of fullest heart" whose "spirit's lovely flame / Nor dazzled nor surprised, because / It always burn'd the same." Perhaps the fact that she was not noticed on the journey down, but merits a dozen lines of glowing appreciation on the way up argues the speaker's increased refinement of perception, for she is "all too beautiful to please / A rash untutor'd taste." But mention concludes here; there is no follow-up—nor was there more in the original version. Champneys has it on good authority that her model was Georgiana Patmore (Emily's younger sister, married in 1854 to Coventry's brother George), "described by one who knew her as a 'sweet, sensible, and in every way most sterling woman, the Ruth of "Tamerton Church Tower."'"[6] If Champneys is correct in another attribution, we have an important statement from Patmore himself about "Tamerton Church-Tower" as the "new Poem" he tells Sutton he is engaged on: "It will be about as long as the 'Ancient Mariner.' I have written two-thirds already. It will be nearly a year before I shall have finished it, for I am anxious to make it very complete."[7] A week later (21 February 1848) Patmore opens another letter to Sutton with "My new poem is to show the right nature—or rather the wrong nature, and through that the right—of love for a woman. It will be my last love poem. . . ."[8]

As for the rest of the *Tamerton Church-Tower* volume, "about seventy [of its 218] pages . . . are altered from 'Poems' published in 1844," we read before the contents page. We look for and find "The Yew-Berry" (once "Lilian"), "The River," "The Falcon," "The Woodman's Daughter," and the "Love's willing page" sonnet. In among these are new poems from work in progress—we will see some later, like "Ladies' Praise" and "Love's Apology," as preludes to various sections of the *Angel in the House*, or like the "Thunder-

Shower," as incidents of the *Victories of Love*. Others are collected from the periodicals which first published them—see chapter 3—"A Sketch in the Manner of Hogarth" (of the crowd at a public hanging), "The Caves of Dahra" (in French Algiers), "The Year" (from the Pre-Raphaelite *Germ*). Changes of title and revisions of text we expect.[9]

II *The Angel in the House*

Coventry Patmore is best known and most often discussed as the author of the heavenly domestic long poem in octosyllabics which has been described as idyl and epic, and which went through several editions during the poet's lifetime.[10] Patmore's first wife, "by whom and for whom [he] became a poet,"[11] was his inspiration, but we must not look for direct portraiture or external biography. And let it be said at the outset that the "Angel" never meant the wife, but rather the spirit of love in Christian marriage.

Each of the two books of the *Angel in the House* has a prologue and twelve cantos. Each canto begins with a few distinct poems thematically related to the narrative part and fulfilling a Greek choric function with reference to it.[12] (In a first encounter with the *Angel* these preludes may get in the modern reader's way.) The two prologues and the epilogue situate the poem fictionally as anniversary gift of the poet to his "ten-years' wife / Whose customary love is not / Her passion, or her play, but life" (*Po*, 207).

The story is a simple one—the serene courtship of the dean's daughter Honoria by Felix Vaughan, a young squire with no special difficulties either of temperament or of circumstances, and its culmination in their wedding and early life together. (A portion of the original prologue excised in subsequent editions had explained that "The Song should have no incidents. . . . Its scope should be the heart's events.")[13] But instead of leaving the Vaughans to live happily ever after, Patmore warms to his thesis in the sequel, the *Victories of Love*,[14] which takes the form of letters between the characters who had entered only the subplot, as it were, of the *Angel*. Frederick Graham, Honoria's cousin, who had hoped vainly for acceptance as a suitor, in his extreme loneliness marries Jane, thoroughly good but intellectually and socially somewhat "beneath" her husband. He gradually comes to appreciate her devotedness before her death, and she is at last made happy in the assurance of his love. The piece concludes with the marriage of the son of Frederick and Jane to the daughter of Felix and Honoria, at which the old dean's wedding sermon provides the vehicle for Patmore's most explicit poetic formulation of his dominant motif.

The *Angel* opens with a conspicuous disclaimer of high style. Felix's "homely Pegasus," he tells his wife, "does but drag a rumbling wain, / Cheer'd by the coupled bells of rhyme." Yet for her sake and "Not careless of the gift of song" he has been meditating a subject for "these last days, the dregs of time." The prologue to book 1, then, besides being the vestibule of the poem, provides a perfectly natural opportunity for announcing the theme and even invoking the Muse, with the genial and permissible exaggeration allowed the fond lover and poet, and whose expectation of renown is like theirs who sang of Laura and of Beatrice:

> "In green and undiscover'd ground,
>   "Yet near where many others sing,
> "I have the very well-head found
>   "Whence gushes the Pierian Spring."
>
> Then she: "What is it, Dear? The Life
>   "Of Arthur, or Jerusalem's Fall?"
> "Neither: your gentle self, my wife,
>   "And love, that grows from one to all."
>
> (Po, 62)

Note the sly, often overlooked but typically Patmorean humor. Honoria is pulling Felix's leg ever so gently (and he self-importantly does not even notice it), playing on the *Morte d'Arthur* and *Jerusalem Delivered* (in the 1854 and 1863 *Betrothal* Felix had loaned Honoria a precious Tasso to read on a railway journey; this eventually became "A Petrarch worth its weight in gold"). Patmore lets Felix poke fun at textual critics:

> "Imagine, Love, how learned men
>   "Will deep-conceiv'd devices find,
> "Beyond my purpose and my ken,
>   "An ancient bard of simple mind.
> "You, sweet, his Mistress, Wife, and Muse,
>   "Were you for mortal woman meant?
> "Your praises give a hundred clues
>   "To mythological intent!

"And severing thus the truth from trope,
    "In you the Commentators see
"Outlines occult of abstract scope,
    "A future for philosophy!"

(*Po*, 62–63)

Felix's speech concludes with a contented reference to the reality around them which embraces their children (like Patmore's own family at the time of writing, two little boys and a baby daughter who, we learn later, is called Emily), the sheep, and "yonder English home" where they "thrive on mortal food and sleep."

She laugh'd. How proud she always was
    To feel how proud he was of her!
But he had grown distraught, because
    The Muse's mood began to stir.

(*Po*, 63)

A separate quatrain, a miniscule fifth strophe of the prologue, achieves the needed transition:

His purpose with performance crown'd,
    He to his well-pleased wife rehears'd,
When next their Wedding-Day came round,
    His leisure's labour, 'Book the First.'

(*Po*, 63)

The preludes to canto 1 reinforce, however unobtrusively, Felix's demand to be read within a recognized literary tradition. When the poet asks "Primal Love, who grantest wings / And voices to the woodland birds" for "the power of saying things / Too simple and too sweet for words" we detect a Victorian approach to the world of Chaucer's *Parliament of Fowles*, where birds of all kinds preened and chattered in the St. Valentine's Day choosing of mates. Chaucer's commission to sing love rightly Patmore had made his own in a way that few contemporary readers related to the great poet of the rhyme royal which Patmore praised[15] but did not imitate. There is veiled allusion to the Dante of both *Commedia* and *Vita Nuova*[16] in "I've travell'd half my worldly course," experienced vanity, remorse, and "how pride may part / Spirits,"

> But have not disbelieved in love;
>   Nor unto love, sole mortal thing
>   Of worth immortal, done the wrong
>   To count it, with the rest that sing,
>   Unworthy of a serious song.

(Po, 64)

Although the third of the three preludes is the most explicit about Patmore's determination to set forth "new truths" which "like new stars, were there / Before, though not yet written down," its scriptural images indicate matter (married love) and manner (sprightly octosyllabics) only by indirection:

> The richest realm of all the earth
>   Is counted still a heathen land,
> Lo, I, like Joshua, now go forth
>   To give it unto Israel's hand.[17]
> .   .   .   .
> Yet, know ye, though my words are gay
>   As David's dance, which Michal scorn'd,
> If kindly you receive the Lay,
>   You shall be sweetly help'd and warn'd.

(Po, 65)

Reminiscence and expectation become expository media in the narrative portions of canto 1. The controlling image of the first strophe is the auspicious "sunny wind," benign and fructifying spirit, that readies all the senses of the protagonist and tunes him in to the harmonious world of the dean's daughters, which, a Cambridge graduate now, he revisits after six years' absence. (Patmore almost went to Cambridge; he also courted the daughter of a Dissenting minister. There is gentle irony in the fact that only his second marriage brought him means to rise to the social and economic level of his ideal Vaughans and Churchills.)

A dozen lines at either end of the canto suffice to show both the consummate skill of Patmore's muted rhetoric and the plain-clothes idealism so often taken for platitude. The symmetry of the first selection, the twelve-line sentence which serves as processional, is remarkable. Lines 1–3 and 10–12 are the protagonist's and balance each other: "I came to Sarum Close" (line 1) and "I reach'd the Dean's" (line 11); and in each triplet the keen anticipation finds a

simple sensory response—to wind, to bells—for focus. Each shows
internal pairing: memory-desire, heart-brain; half-half, trembled-
trembling. The middle six lines belong to the wind whose versatility
is revealed in the parallel "And" plus verb which begins each of the
six, and in the variously modified objects ending each; similar con-
structions link the ends of 5 with 6, and 7 with 8, while 4 and 9 are
mirror images.

> Once more I came to Sarum Close,
>   With joy half memory, half desire,
> And breathed the sunny wind that rose
>   And blew the shadows o'er the Spire,
> And toss'd the lilac's scented plumes,
>   And sway'd the chestnut's thousand cones,
> And fill'd my nostrils with perfumes,
>   And shaped the clouds in waifs and zones,
> And wafted down the serious strain
>   Of Sarum bells, when, true to time,
> I reach'd the Dean's, with heart and brain
>   That trembled to the trembling chime.
>
> (*Po*, 66)

Light, scent, and sound converge to the moment "true to time" for
the first instance, not just of time-chime rhyme, but of the motif of
church bell as symbol of order at peaks of emotional intensity.[18]

The dean's family and fireside, his deceased wife and three fair
daughters, come into the foreground with flashback and description
building up into a tangible embodiment of the values Patmore set
store by, gently here and ferociously in the political odes. The canto
concludes:

> For something that abode endued
>   With temple-like repose, an air
> Of life's kind purposes pursued
>   With ordered freedom sweet and fair.
> A tent pitch'd in a world not right
>   It seem'd, whose inmates, every one,
> On tranquil faces bore the light
>   Of duties beautifully done,
> And humbly, though they had few peers,
>   Kept their own laws, which seem'd to be
> The fair sum of six thousand years'
>   Traditions of civility.
>
> (*Po*, 69)

Here is contrast with the concrete, sensorily imaged, syntactically simple opening lines. Abstract and slightly sinuous, the passage demonstrates another string to Patmore's bow. Verbs devoid of action ("endued," "seem'd," "bore," "kept") support the impression of stability, and even if the "six thousand years"—surely a slip for "six hundred," since British "traditions of civility" dating from nearly 4,000 B.C. would be very riskily involved—take us back to the century of the Magna Carta, the heritage Patmore honors here is less that of rough barons than of their gracious ladies. (Again, in the *Victories of Love*, Patmore turns to "women beautiful and wise, / With England's greatness in their eyes"—*Po*, 285.)

Considerations of space preclude a detailed examination of each canto, but a prelude to the second, containing Patmore's personal statement of purpose as poet, "to raise . . . a worthy hymn in woman's praise," suggests an important digression. He is the heir of Sidney and the Golden World critics for whom art improves on nature: ". . . geranium, pink, or rose / Is thrice itself through power of art" (*Po*, 71), and he frankly intends to "teach how noble man should be." A clarifying essay years later calls poetry "persuasive music assisting commanding truth to convince" and goes on to explain:

> The advocate of art for "the emotions and the emotions only," cannot be brought to understand that the alternative is not "didactic" art, which is as much a contradiction in terms as his own notion of art is. Of great and beautiful things beauty and greatness are the only proofs and expressions; and the ideas of the greatest artists are the morality of a sphere too pure and high for "didactic" teaching. The teaching of art is the suggestion—far more convincing than assertion—of an ethical science, the germs of which are to the mass of mankind incommunicable. . . .[19]

The poet, like the social reformer, the natural philosopher, the cynical humorist, has his distinct function, viz., to affirm "things which it greatly concerns men to know, but which they have either not discovered or have allowed to lapse into the death of commonplace."[20]

Patmore's affirmations are woven industriously in narrative and prelude with threads of observation and tradition, fact and fancy, humor and idealism, experience and theory. For a brief space canto 2 lets us believe that a romance may develop between Felix and the middle daughter, Mary. But she shows him a set of her verses on consolation after dryness in prayer, and "well she knew that I knew well / Her grace with silence to requite." At lunch immediately afterward the youngest, Mildred, moves into first place among the sixteen prior or potential lady loves Felix reviews mentally: ". . . in London two, / Two at Bowness, in Paris none [is this a belated repudiation of the youthful Coventry's cruel Miss Gore?] / And, last and best, in Sarum three." With true Patmorean economy, by the end of the canto "I could but note / Honoria, less admired the while, / Was lovelier, though from love remote" (*Po*, 74–76). Henceforth there is no deviation, and the symptoms of the courtly lover appear:

> Her beauty haunts him all the night;
> It melts his heart, it makes him weep
> For wonder, worship, and delight.
>
> (*Po*, 77)

With a fresher touch, "He prays for some hard thing to do . . . though he merits not / to kiss the braid upon her skirt. . . ." Characteristically Patmore avoids a scriptural cliché like the hem of her garment and calls attention to a detail of Victorian dressmaking: "the braid upon her skirt" is not the trimming but the braid or cording customarily sewn into the bottom edge where skirt and lining join, to save the long skirt from wearing out too quickly as it brushes the ground.

Patmore in many passages distinguishes lofty spiritual love from corrupt passion. One aphoristic quatrain prompted by a hypothetical "wasteful woman" is worth quoting for its Pope-like neatness (Patmore less often achieves such meaningful compression in his couplets):

> How given for nought her priceless gift,
> How spoil'd the bread and spill'd the wine,
> Which, spent with due, respective thrift,
> Had made brutes men, and men divine.
>
> (*Po*, 79)

This is an early statement of the sacramentality of love, human love symbolic of divine, a concept that develops in Patmore's thinking and experience to the pitch attained in the later odes.[21] That Patmore is all of a piece can be seen by parallel citations. Intuitions about the spiritual life and even about virginity as a value are tentatively voiced by Mary Churchill in the *Angel in the House* and the *Victories of Love* (therefore by 1863) and crystallized in the sometimes ecstatic prose of *The Rod, the Root, and the Flower* in 1895, for example:

Man and woman are as the charcoal poles of the electric light, lifeless in themselves, but, in conjunction, the vehicles of and sharers in the fire and splendour which burst forth from the embrace of the original duality of Love, in the double-tongued flames of Pentecost. They are modes and means of God's fruition of Himself in Nature, and the more they confess and discern their own nullity, the greater will be their share in his power of felicity. (*R*, 114)

The introduction of Frederick Graham as potential rival is treated with the sympathetic humor that Patmore had evinced as early as the 1844 "Sir Hubert." The touch of mock-heroic is perfectly blended with psychological realism and deft metaphor in nature description as the restless lover finally drops off to sleep:

> As drowsiness my brain reliev'd,
>   A shrill defiance of all to arms,
> Shriek'd by the stable-cock, receiv'd
>   An angry answer from three farms.
> And, then, I dream'd that I, her knight,
>   A clarion's haughty pathos heard,
> And rode securely to the fight,
>   Cased in the scarf she had conferr'd;
> And there, the bristling lists behind,
>   Saw many, and vanquish'd all I saw
> Of her unnumber'd cousin-kind,
>   In Navy, Army, Church, and Law.
>
>   (*Po*, 81–82)

Patmore's rhetoric in ladies' praise exhibits every device of *amplificatio* in the manuals. One litany of how-plus-adjective phrases (amiable, candid, sweet, etc.) includes a truly Augustan turn: "How able her persuasions are / To prove, her reasons to persuade" (*Po*, 84), and sweeps on to extravagant Nature's tribute: "Whatever runs, flies, lives, or delves, / All doff for her their ornaments, / Which suit her better than themselves" (*Po*, 85).

Had Patmore's early critics noticed that he was wearing the mask of Felix, virtuoso and householder, they might have enjoyed more the in-character rightness of the "kid-glove verses" of "an honourable man who mistakes huckaback for damask." So spoke the *Athenaeum* after carrying Henry Fothergill Chorley's review-parody (which was not surpassed by Swinburne's *Heptalogia* later on):

The gentle reader we apprise That this new "Angel in the House" contains a tale not very wise About a person and a spouse. The author, gentle as a lamb,

Has managed his rhymes to fit, and, haply, fancies he has writ Another "In Memoriam." How his intended gathered flowers, And took her tea and after sung, Is told in style somewhat like ours, for delectation of the young. . . . The rest will come another day if public sympathy allows, And this is all we have to say, About "The Angel in the House."[22]

When the *Critic* greeted the third part of the *Angel, Faithful For Ever* (1860), with "Mr. Coventry Patmore threatens to become an institution. . . . if we are to have angels in the house every year . . . it really will *not* do," Ruskin came to Patmore's defense in the next issue. He admits apparent shortcomings—"places of rest, or of dead colour; or of intended harshness"—in "a finished and tender work of very noble art," and cites in justification Homer's plain description of Nausicaa's washing in contrast with Pope's dressed up version of the same.[23] One who objects to "Our witnesses the Cook and Groom" (*Po*, 87) or "The ladies rose, I held the door" (*Po*, 97) may recall "No fear lest Dinner cool" in *Paradise Lost* (bk. 5, line 396). It is easier to find examples of poignant tenderness like "His only Love, and she is wed! / His fondness comes about his heart, / As milk comes when the babe is dead" (*Po*, 134).

Patmore's ups and downs are not unimportant to our consideration, although a large measure of his contemporary popularity rested on qualities other than his poetic excellence; he was valued for sound morals and homely wisdom, and preeminently for portraying the ideal of Victorian womanhood. That he was always artist and craftsman meant more to himself than to most of his readers, yet his endless tampering with the text seems often to be for the sake of making matter and meter more bland to the sensibilities and smooth to the ear, for example, "That Male and Female are the poles / On which the spheres of joy revolve"[24] becomes "The nuptial contrasts are the poles / On which the heavenly spheres revolve" (*Po*, 72) and "I never would sully my faith" (*AB*, 66) eases into "That I would never dim my faith" (*Po*, 87).

It takes Felix six cantos from the time he secures the dean's consent until he finds suitable opportunity to ask Honoria to marry him, but the actual proposal is dispatched with brevity and delicacy and without direct quotation—"Twice rose, twice died my trembling word"; then intense consciousness of the cathedral chimes and of her physical presence, "And, oh, sweet meeting of desires, / She, answering, own'd that she loved too" (*Po*, 136).

The unsentimental psychological realist then comes through— "The summit won, I paused and sigh'd, / As if success itself had

fail'd"—and the fiancée, too, "By love unsceptred," has to adjust to
her new role and reassert "The honour of her vanquish'd heart" by
maidenly reserve at the next meeting. Likewise, at the actual wedding near the end of book 2,

> Life smitten with a feverish chill,
>   The brain too tired to understand,
> In apathy of heart and will,
>   I took the woman from the hand
> Of him who stood for God, and heard
>   Of Christ, and of the Church his Bride.
>
> (*Po*, 197)

The small, external, all human events of the final canto—"How
light the touches are that kiss / The music from the chords of life!"—
are therefore no letdown from a state of euphoria but a preview of the
quiet felicity which the epilogue reflects more largely as of ten years
later. Also, by reintroducing cousin Frederick, one time rival, now
"unselfish to a fault" (Felix thinks, "if fate, / Unfair, had only fashion'd
me / As hapless, I had been as great"), the poet points to the sequel,
The *Victories of Love*.

III   The Victories of Love

Patmore had originally planned The *Angel in the House* in six
books, but wrote only four: *The Betrothal, The Espousals, Faithful
For Ever*, and *The Victories of Love*. These, published separately
between 1854 and 1862, appeared in two volumes in 1863. Since then
the title *Angel in the House* usually applies to books 1 and 2, and
Victories of Love to books 3 and 4, with the last two books referred to
as books 1 and 2 of the *Victories of Love*.

In these last Patmore has set himself a different task. In the *Angel*
he had spoken through the poet Vaughan even when Vaughan was not
speaking as the first-person protagonist. The point of view was single,
or naively ventriloquist. In the *Victories of Love* there is no containing or mediating structure, only a series of letters by several hands.
The focus of the multiple points of view is, to be sure, marriage. We
see Felix's and Honoria's wedded life still blissful after twenty years.
We consider Mary Churchill's renunciation of matrimony. We are
shown Frederick's and Jane's marriage as it ultimately works out and
is seen by them, by Frederick's wisdom-dispensing mother, or by the
refreshingly "worldly" Lady Clitheroe (little Mildred Churchill
grown up).

But by a curious delaying tactic the reader almost simulates Frederick's two-year voyage at the end of which, halfway through book I, he discovers that Honoria and Felix are already wed. Our literary occupation meanwhile is ingenious. Frederick's octosyllabic couplets (eight of the first ten letters are his) not only review his condition as hopeless lover, recalling the standard features of such a hero, but include a variety of other elements. There is Wordsworthian reminiscence: when the spell of an earlier love had converted the rough boy to gentleness

> No more the unnested blackbird's shriek
> Startled the light-leaved wood; on high
> Wander'd the gadding butterfly,
> Unscared by my flung cap. . . .
>
> (*Po*, 212)

There are readily transposable bits of description (we have already seen salvaged sections of earlier poems incorporated here):

> Waves scud to shore against the wind
> That flings the sprinkling surf behind;
> In port the bickering pennons show
> Which way the ships would gladly go;
> Through Edgecumb Park the rooted trees
> Are tossing, reckless, in the breeze. . . .
>
> (*Po*, 219)

Here one thinks back to "Tamerton Church-Tower"; one even thinks ahead to A. E. Housman's "On Wenlock Edge," and remembers that Housman admired Patmore.[25] There are patriotic portions:

> Yonder, at last, the glad sea roars
> Along the sacred English shores!
> There lies the lovely land I know,
> Where men and women lordliest grow;
> . . . .
> There curls the wanton cottage smoke
> Of him that drives but bears no yoke. . . .
>
> (*Po*, 237)

And there are dreams and fantasies, perhaps the least plausible ingredients in letters even from a lonely man at sea to a mother in whom he confides.

The action, or at least the change of state, begins when Frederick in letter twelve blurts out that he has married Jane; "*such* a girl!" says Lady Clitheroe to Mary Churchill, "Her Mother was a Kitchen-Maid." (This rumor is retracted later when Jane charms all by her complete simplicity.) Jane next enters the correspondence, admitting to her mother her initial misery and wishing with utter sincerity that "he had that fancied Wife, / With me for Maid, now!" When Frederick reports the arrival of their baby and the consequent dawning of real tenderness in himself, a happier cycle begins, although it is only on the eve of Jane's death that Frederick realizes how deeply he loves her. We are probably overprepared for this, with Patmore's bent in this direction already established, and Mrs. Graham senior's prophetic letter (she had also warned too late of the impending rebound marriage—"Wed not one woman, oh, my Child, / Because another has not smiled," (*Po*, 243). Yet Jane's last letter to Frederick, biographically close to Emily Augusta's to Coventry, has some genuinely moving passages and wise advice:

> Grieve with the heart; let not the head
> Grieve on, when grief of heart is dead;
> For all the powers of life defy
> A superstitious constancy.
> . . . .
> And should it chance as it may be,
> Give her my wedding ring from me. . . .
>
> (*Po*, 299)

In the practical delicacy of her love Jane assures Frederick that he need not reproach himself for his taciturnity or moodiness in the early days of their marriage when she "really did behave / So stupidly" and compared so poorly with Honoria; she gives him the good news of their John's acceptance by Honoria's Emily; with a very sure touch she tells him this is the perfect time for her to die, and he can say "Love an eternal temper took, / Dipp'd glowing, in death's icy brook!"

This eighth of the thirteen letters in book 2 thus gives a new impetus to life in its sense of happy fulfillment of one kind of relationship, and in its expectation of good things to come for those Jane leaves behind. In the rapid glimpses that follow we take Lady Clitheroe's word for the beautiful wedding and for Frederick's determination to go to sea again now that it's over. She has incisive comments about bringing up daughters (Honoria has proved the wiser after all) and conducting a household. She is penetrating, not unkind, when she replies to Mrs. Graham: "You say Fred never writes to you / Frankly, as once he used to do, / About himself; and you complain / He shared with none his grief for Jane. / . . . Honoria, to whose heart alone / He seems to open all his own, / At times has tears in her kind eyes, / After their private colloquies" (*Po*, 302). Frederick himself writes to Honoria of heavenly felicity and faithful love "Not on the changeful earth alone" (*Po*, 305), with an ambiguous Jacob and Rachel reference that either casts Jane as Leah or has some Swedenborgian resolution that Patmore decided not to explore at this time.

Richer in pathos and more rarely humorous, the two books of the *Victories of Love* made less stir than the *Angel*'s two. The novelty of Patmore's "epic" had of course worn off, and their epistolary form made the *Victories* more obviously didactic. Only prior prowling in the early and unreprinted poems discovers the extent to which Patmore cut and pasted in what is actually a highly presentable work although seen through the press under the strain and weariness of approaching and realized widowerhood. He could also have felt his octosyllabics growing stale and a new mode ready to be grasped after a respite.

The *Wedding Sermon* which ends the *Victories of Love* points clearly to the odes. Terence Connolly, S.J., the Boston College scholar and librarian who began the Patmore collection (as well as the Thompson and the Meynell) observes: "The truths of 'The Wedding Sermon' are cold and measured and restrained. The same truths in the odes are warm with passion, intimate, and poured forth with the abandon that marks all great lyric poetry."[26] The difference is partly accounted for but not minimized by realizing the persons and the formal occasion of the sermon-poem, Dean Churchill preaching at his granddaughter's wedding.

The boldness of Patmore's analogies of marriage and the spiritual life comes through early in the poem when he compares a temporary loss of zest for nuptial duties to the withdrawal of sensible devotion in prayer; there are striking parallels between Patmorean insights and the findings of traditional mystical writers. Patmore was much impressed by the life and writings of Marie Lataste which he could have read in an 1862 French edition.[27]

Section 5 of the *Wedding Sermon* relates virginity to marriage as an initial counsel of restraint "given that lovers never may / Be without sacrifice to lay / On the high altar of true love," for "To move / Frantic,

like comets to our bliss," would mar a relationship which is enhanced
by "Seeking for aye, without alloy / Of selfish thought, another's joy, /
And finding in degrees unknown / That which in act they shunn'd,
their own." A simple statement of Patmore's principle follows: "all
delights of earthly love / Are shadows of the heavens, and move / As
other shadows do; they flee / From him that follows them" (*Po*, 325).

The sermon ends with typical Patmorean emphasis on the development of love and deepening of union through the right use of
marriage: "the body's bond / Is all else utterly beyond / In power of
love to actualise / The soul's bond which it signifies" (*Po*, 336).

We are reminded of Donne's "Extasie." This is the sort of un-
Victorian directness that made Aubrey De Vere, Newman, Housman,
and others among Patmore's friends and readers cringe. But it is a
note he not only insisted on playing but pointed vigorously to the
scriptural precedent for, and total orthodoxy of, which of course no
one contested. To a later readership he speaks with greater
understanding.

CHAPTER 5

The Odes

THE odes may well be the best way to Patmore for the modern reader, although one would be hard put to prove that they are intrinsically superior to the *Angel* where Patmore is master of the terse rather than dispenser of the lavish. The greater accessibility of the apparently free form, and the sustained passion even of the political odes, are an invitation to share the poet's experience less encumbered by the discreet formality of the narrative quatrains and couplets.

The title, *The Unknown Eros*, applies at all stages to the growing sequence of poems in Patmore's new manner: the privately printed (1868) original nine *Odes* (withdrawn and destroyed after two years of uncertain reception); the holograph manuscript (in the British Library) of fourteen (with accompanying proof sheets of the second published edition and a note by Coventry on Swinburne's and Tennyson's "borrowings" from him before his own poems appeared in book form); the editions of 1877 (thirty-one poems) and 1878 (forty-six poems); the final two-book arrangement of twenty-four plus eighteen odes on a variety of subjects—sponsal love, human bereavement, union with God, political corruption, and the role of the elect. J. C. Reid goes to some trouble to persuade us, against "those who read it on publication as a miscellany, with no unity of idea or conception," that the *Unknown Eros* "is as complex and as serious a work as was written in England in the nineteenth century. It speaks to the twentieth century with a clearer voice than it spoke to Patmore's own age. The marks of strain and tension in it, and the struggle towards personal integration, give it an immediacy which most contemporary readers fail to find in Browning or Tennyson."[1]

Whether or not Frederick Page was correct in assigning the widower's poems to Frederick Graham and the political "speeches" to Felix Vaughan in a tentative reconstruction of the abandoned "final section [of the *Angel in the House*] on the subject of the hope which remains for individual love in death,"[2] there is no reason to insist on discontinuity in Patmore's new-appearing work in altered circumstances.

Nature, love, society, truth, penitence, virginity, and the spiritual life are Reid's categories for a good running presentation of the proem and forty-two odes of the ultimate *Unknown Eros* plus a few poems no longer in the *Eros* sequence but retained in the Patmore canon.

The Latin epigraph of the 1877 *Unknown Eros*, Wisdom speaking in Proverbs (8:31), translates: "My delight is to be with the children of men." This is the setting and pitch for the harmonious interaction of divine and human love of which Patmore is about to sing in a new way. But the "Proem" categorizes "Love's three-stranded ray" as "Red wrath, compassion golden, lazuline delight" (*Po*, 347), and itself starts out on the first strand, because "weary of the greatness of her ways, / There lies my Land, . . . / Her ancient beauty marr'd," with only the "ghostly grace of her transfigured past" to bequeath to "nations yet unborn." With "Uranian Clearness" and "Notes few and strong and fine" like "a lonely thrush's" the poet hopes to transcend or at least "wash away / With tears" disfiguring "dust and stain."

I   Unknown Eros, *Book 1*

"Saint Valentine's Day" (book 1, ode 1), anticipating brighter May "When all things meet to marry" (*Po*, 351), brings out paradox and complementarity through the safe medium of nature imagery. The "quick, praevernal Power" stirs the snowdrop to flower, "Fair as the rash oath of virginity / Which is first-love's first cry." Immediately then the poet invokes "Baby Spring, / That flutter'st 'neath the breast of Earth / A month before the birth." This still secret life and not yet manifest force is questioned about the "joy contrite, / Sadder than sorrow, sweeter than delight, / That burthens now the breath of everything," and is exemplified concretely and specifically in dawn and evening birdsong and in human nostalgia. The suggested answer, the tension between renunciation and fulfillment, tips the balance in favor of love's "soft ecstasy," but the lingering consideration of "waked Earth . . . / Uttering first-love's first cry, / Vainly renouncing, with a Seraph's sigh, / Love's natural hope" preserves the ambivalence of Patmore's attitude in his second marriage and toward his daughter's vocation to vowed virginity (she had entered the convent five years before this poem was first published in 1878).

In "Wind and Wave" (book 1, ode 2), although it first appeared in the 1877 *Unknown Eros*, Terence Connolly sees a sequel, as summer consummation, to the preceding spring poem. Without quarreling with this reading, for the "wedded light and heat" do beget the violet, we can also see the poem as a fuller exploration of the virginity theme. The model, Mary's motherhood, is presented in the question, "Is the One found, / . . . To make Heaven's bound" (*Po*, 353), rather like the scriptural "Who is this arising like the dawn, fair as the moon, resplendent as the sun, terrible as an army with banners?" (*Song of Songs*, 6:10). The stress is on the manner of her conceiving: "So that in Her / All which it hath of sensitively good / Is sought and understood / After the narrow mode the mighty Heavens prefer?" The last half of the poem is a particularly good text to illustrate Patmore's felicitous control of rhythm and image reinforcing each other, his self-resolving tensions, his power to suggest simultaneously the vitality of sex and sex transcended.

> She, as a little breeze
> Following still Night,
> Ripples the spirit's cold, deep seas
> Into delight;
> But, in a while,
> The immeasurable smile
> Is broke by fresher airs to flashes blent
> With darkling discontent;
> And all the subtle zephyr hurries gay,
> And all the heaving ocean heaves one way,
> 'Tward the void sky-line and an unguess'd weal;
> Until the vanward billows feel
> The agitating shallows, and divine the goal,
> And to foam roll,
> And spread and stray
> And traverse wildly, like delighted hands,
> The fair and fleckless sands;
> And so the whole
> Unfathomable and immense
> Triumphing tide comes at the last to reach
> And burst in wind-kiss'd splendours on the deaf'ning beach,
> Where forms of children in first innocence
> Laugh and fling pebbles on the rainbow'd crest
> Of its untired rest.
>
> (*Po*, 353–54)

There are literary half-echoes—we catch the smile of Beatrice, and Matthew Arnold's darkling plain where a decade or so earlier ignorant armies clashed by night now seems Dover Beach by daylight, and the pebbles flung by laughing children have lost their grating roar.

To make a four-season sequence (as Reid and Connolly wish) "L'Allegro" would have to be lifted from the 1878 *Amelia* volume and put between "Wind and Wave" and "Winter" in the *Eros*. But "dreaming field and bossy Autumn wood" (*Po*, 461) are viewed from a "thou art young, and I am gray" position that is both scornful and complacent: "Science, beyond all other lust / Endow'd with appetite for dust, / We glance at where it grunts, well-sty'd, / And pass upon the other side"—"And now come home. / Where none of our mild days / Can fail, though simple, to confess / The magic of mysteriousness" (*Po*, 463). The "thou" of the poem is at once abstract "Felicity," twin sister of "Certitude," and the concrete "Dearest" whom the speaker asks "Is't Love or Friendship . . . we obey?" Quite possibly the husband was the middle-aged lover of Amelia in the preceding poem. She is now the mother of the "charming Wonders three" mentioned at the poem's end. The couple walk around an estate like Heron's Ghyll complete with trout, partridges, and hay stacks "Under our pleased and prosperous eyes." Patmore's final placing of this poem is definitely in the story line which would make "Amelia" and "L'Allegro" the ghost of another *Angel in the House*.

"Amelia," privately printed in 1878, became later that year the title poem of a new Patmore collection: *Amelia, Tamerton Church-Tower, etc., with a Prefatory Study of English Metrical Law*.[3] The six-page poem, one of Patmore's favorites, resembles in form and size the longer *Psyche* odes, but runs as a simple narrative with snatches of conversation and passages of reflective description. It is a very local poem, obviously set in Hastings, "the little, bright, surf-breathing town" with its gardens "scatter[ed]" up the sunny southern slope to the "gorse-lit shoulder of the down / That keeps the north-wind from the nestling town." The sea can be glimpsed from the Ridge (the upper road) and also in "turning a dim street" in Old Hastings where between two cliffs the Conqueror's harbor once bit deeper into the land.

The action is simple. Amelia and her patient lover, the "I" of the poem, visit the grave of his "once-betrothed, Millicent." His "superior age" and Amelia's childlikeness make natural and unembarrassed their praise of the dead and Amelia's accepting to wear "for *her* sake" the "band / Of mildest pearls" which had been Millicent's. The endearments are gentle and the understanding complete. Going out and return is a movement from urgency to peace. The perfectly controlled tone of the poem and the rightness of its diction show the poet's mastery better than his more "striking" pieces do.

"Winter" (book 1, ode 3), the last of the nature odes, personifies Patmore's favorite season in an unobtrusive way; the "pallor on her face . . . is not death, but plenitude of peace" near the beginning, and at the end she has a "look of exile from some great repose." The poet perceives "less the characters of dark and cold / Than warmth and light asleep," and testifies with familiar images of the small or unborn child—"the infant harvest, breathing soft below / Its eider coverlet of snow" and "Winter's sometime smiles, that seem to well / From infancy ineffable"—and with quite a catalog of flowers asserting themselves in occasional thaws. The poem both pulses with the promise of life and sustains the impression of peace it began by explicitating.

"Beata" (book 1, ode 4) is a very short poem having as single image the spectrum which mediates the overpowering white light of heaven in the beloved, "Nothing of Heaven in thee showing infinite, / Save the delight." "The Day after Tomorrow" (ode 5) deals with the re-union of lovers (spouses)—"One day's controlled hope, and then one more, / And on the third our lives shall be fulfill'd" as often before with "One sweet drop more, in absolute increase / Of unrelapsing peace" (*Po*, 357). In "Tristitia" (ode 6) the uxorious lover exacts a promise of his lady that she will nor grieve if she be saved and he, "beguiled by gracious-seeming sin, / Say, loving too much thee," be condemned to "that dateless exile gray / . . . named in surpliced Schools *Tristitia*;" his weal is secure insofar as she is happy.

The next few poems are more specifically narrative-autobiographical. In the often anthologized "Azalea" (book 1, ode 7), the widower wakes from dreaming his wife is dead only to recall that she is so in reality. "Departure" (ode 8) poignantly recollects "that July afternoon" when "with sudden, unintelligible phrase, / And frighten'd eye" the dying wife went her "journey of all days," abruptly at the last, and "all unlike [her] great and gracious ways."[4] "Eurydice" (ode 9) is a strangely modern poem amid these restrained if not conventional expressions of mourning. Its nightmare search "Thro' sordid streets and lanes / . . . And infamous doors, opening on hapless rooms" gives grief a bitterly realistic edge. With "The Toys" (ode 10) we return to the anthologized domestic in the motherless naughty boy's "lesson" to the stern father of God's mercy on our childishness. "Tired Memory" (ode 11), which was one of the original nine odes privately printed in 1868, has in its painful honesty an impact which does not lose its freshness: "The stony rock of death's insensibility / Well'd yet awhile with honey of thy love / And then was dry" (*Po*, 366). The themes of "Eurydice"and "Tristitia" recur, delicately modulated, then "a strange grace of thee / In a fair stranger . . . / . . . bade the wheels to stir / Of sensitive delight in the poor brain, / Dead of devotion and tired memory, / So that I lived again" (*Po*, 369).

The remaining odes of book 1 are two more bereavement poems, four "public" utterances, and seven prophetic-spiritual pieces. "'If I were dead, you'd sometimes say, Poor Child!'" is the first of the sixteen lines of ode 14 (entitled simply "'If I Were Dead'") which uses "Poor Child," alone or repeated, as a refrain line four times. This circumstance, and the brevity, limited rhyming, and sprightly filled out rhythms of the poem faintly (and not too happily) suggest a rondel or other stylized French form. Ode 16, "A Farewell"—"With all my will, but much against my heart, / We two now part"—is considered by Terence Connolly to be "Patmore's valedictory to his dead wife's religious faith and to the former unity of belief he shared with her."[5] (She had feared he would become a Catholic.) This may be so despite the twelve-year gap betwwen conversion and first publication,[6] but as in the earlier poems we have no mandate to push biographical identification too far.

"Magna Est Veritas" (ode 12) launches the political odes in ten temperate lines that would actually make a dignified finale as well as a neat demonstration of harmonious rhythm and image:

> Here, in this little Bay,
> Full of tumultuous life and great repose,
> Where, twice a day,
> The purposeless, glad ocean comes and goes,
> Under high cliffs, and far from the huge town,
> I sit me down.
> For want of me the world's course will not fail:
> When all its work is done, the lie shall rot;
> The truth is great, and shall prevail,
> When none cares whether it prevail or not.
>
> (*Po*, 369)

This is the only ode that lacks a publication note in Connolly. It is not one of the original nine, nor does it seem to have appeared in the *Pall Mall Gazette* prior to its inclusion in the 1877 *Unknown Eros*. Here, as in "Wind and Wave," we catch a echo-in-reverse of Matthew Arnold ("Dover Beach" was published in 1867), although to be sure the cliffs are Hastings, not Dover.

"1867" (ode 13), the last of the original nine odes, takes its title from the year of the second Reform Bill, which Patmore deplored as "disfranchising" the middle and upper classes because it extended the suffrage to some three million new voters. His views on this "great crime" of the "false English Nobles and their Jew" (Disraeli and Gladstone both come heavily under the irrational censure of the poet-as-prophet), on the "outlaw'd Best," "sordid Trader," "Mechanic vain," and "orgies of the multitude" splutter through to a scourge-of-God conclusion which may yet bring "to the humbled Earth the Time of Grace." With a reminiscence of Clough, Patmore bids

> Christ's own look through
> The darkness, suddenly increased,
> To the gray secret lingering in the East.
>
> (*Po*, 372)

"Peace" (ode 15) is equally embarrassing as it tells "the sleepy mongers of false ease / That war's the ordained way of all alive" (*Po*, 374), but nothing caps "1880—85" (ode 17, spanning the 1884 Reform Bill) with its reference to Gladstone as the

> Leader, lusting to be seen.
> His leprosy's so perfect that men call him clean!
> Listen the long, sincere, and liberal bray
> Of the earnest Puller at another's hay
> 'Gainst aught that dares to tug the other way.
>
> (*Po*, 379)

This is the temper of much of the late prose, too, that Patmore insists on reprinting in *Religio Poetae* and *Principle in Art*.

We turn with some relief to the last seven poems of book 1. They are not without Patmorean eccentricity:

> The Universe, outside our living Earth,
> Was all conceiv'd in the Creator's mirth,
> Forecasting at the time Man's spirit deep,
> To make dirt cheap.
>
> (*Po*, 381)

"The Two Deserts" (ode 18, on outer space and the microscopic world) reveals the concrete imagination still powerful if a bit macabre: the "Moon's fair ball" is "A corpse in Night's highway,

naked, fire-scarr'd, accurst," while "the minutest water-drop" contains "A torment of innumerable tails" (Po, 382); the poet recommends ordinary vision. "The bitter jest / Of mankind's progress" (Po,
383) haunts Patmore in "Crest and Gulf" (ode 19), but "Let Be!" (ode
20) leaves off judging: "Another is mistook / Through his deceitful
likeness to his look!" (Po, 385). "Faint Yet Pursuing" (ode 21), one of
the original nine, uses as title the phrase describing Gideon's army
(Judges 8:4) which Patmore five years before had told his daughter
Emily was his personal motto.[7] Yet even the humbling realization
"That less than highest is good, and may be high" is not without
smugness:

> An even walk in life's uneven way,
> Though to have dreamt of flight and not to fly
> Be strange and sad,
> Is not a boon that's given to all who pray.
>
> (Po, 385–86)

"Victory in Defeat" (ode 22) at first comes more profoundly to grips
with the experience of one's own inadequacy, but at the end has God
commending the persevering fighter above Joshua in Jericho with

> ". . . lo, the glad surprise
> Of peace beyond surmise,
> More than in common Saints, for ever in his eyes."
>
> (Po, 389)

"Remembered Grace" (ode 23) still deals with the elect, "Whom God
does once with heart to heart befriend," and whose soul on that
account remains constant "When all the other idiot people" are
deceived. The scriptural image of ode 24, "Vesica Piscis," is either
double or confused. The disciples "labour'd through the Night" in
vain and then took a big catch with the first morning net at the
Master's bidding; on a different occasion the disputed tribute coin
was found in a fish ordered caught for just this purpose. Patmore's
appropriation of the fisherman's success is in terms of his capturing
the Lord who speaks through the poet "of forgotten things to far-off
times to come," and not to the common herd today!
    Even Emily had reservations about some of her father's state-
ments: "You must be expecting to hear about the Odes before now,"
she writes on 14 April 1878 from her convent at St. Leonards, the next
town to Hastings where her family lived.

If I say anything foolish, you must remember that I am one of the "hare-brained brood" you mention [in "Crest and Gulf"]. St. Peter says of St. Paul's Epistles that there are in them certain things hard to be understood, which many unlearned and unstable wrest, as they do the other Scriptures, to their own destruction. I think that might be said of the Odes,—"Remembered Grace," for instance. . . .[8]

However it was not so much the distasteful arrogance of some of the odes of Book 1 that contemporaries like Aubrey De Vere objected to, but rather the mystical marriage odes of Book 2 of *The Unknow Eros* with their sexual imagery that is more like the *Song of Songs* than D. G. Rossetti and the "Fleshly School."

II Unknown Eros, *Book 2*

Book 2 opens on a very different note from the gloom and righte-ousness of the preceding pages. Ode 1, "To the Unknown Eros," rises as though on the queried wings "Through delicatest ether feathering soft their solitary beat" to approach a new experience, "A bond I know not of nor dimly can divine" (*Po*, 392, 393). The poet asks, "What God . . . Art Thou?" "Not Amor," nor Diana "mooned Queen of Maids" but transcending both, and inviting the dancer into the "double-center'd circuit" where the enigma of fulfillment through renunciation rests:

> "There lies the crown
> Which all thy longing cures.
> Refuse it, Mortal, that it may be yours!"
>
> (*Po*, 394)

It would seem to be ode 2, "The Contract," that prompted Charles Williams to say "the nearest Miltonic poet to Milton was Patmore; in fact, Patmore might be described as Milton without Satan."[9] Pat-more's Eve, invited to the bridal bed, replies:

> "My Lord, my Wisdom, nay!
> Does not yon love-delighted Planet run,
> (Haply against her heart,)
> A space apart
> For ever from her strong-persuading Sun!
> O say,
> Shall we no voluntary bars
> Set to our drift? I, Sister of the Stars,
> And Thou, my glorious, course-compelling Day!"
>
> (*Po*, 395)

Adam realizes that he should have thought of this first, and accepts the responsibility when Eve says:

board 90

> Be as Archangel Michael's severing sword!"
>
> *(Po,* 396)

The conversation over, the poet sums up:

> Thus the first Eve
> With much enamour'd Adam did enact
> Their mutual free contract
> Of virgin spousals, blissful beyond flight
> Of modern thought. . . .
>
> *(Po,* 397)

The poem's conclusion makes clear what it has been leading up to, the never completed work on the marriage of the Blessed Virgin,

> a heaven-caress'd and happier Eve
> . . . join'd with some glad Saint
> In like espousals . . .
>
> *(Po,* 397)

and ultimately

> No numb, chill-hearted, shaken-witted thing,
> 'Plaining his little span,
> But of proud virgin joy the appropriate birth,
> The Son of God and Man.
>
> *(Po,* 397)

"Arbor Vitae" and "The Standards" (odes 3 and 4) are poems of another stamp that understandably distressed Patmore's gentler champions. The Tree of Life is the Church, overgrown, scarred by storms, "thick with nests of the hoarse bird / That talks, but understands not his own word," yet still bearing good fruit in rough rind "rejected by the forest-pigs"; at its foot "Sits, Tartar-like, the Time's civility, / And eats its dead-dog off a golden dish" (*Po,* 398). The "Standards" begins militantly, as against Gladstone's anti-Catholic pamphlet after the first Vatican Council. Newman's band is "the light" that "Shines from the solitary peak at Edgbaston" (the uphill suburb where the Birmingham Oratory was). Some of Patmore's complaints sound not unlike those of many a conservative Catholic after Vatican II:

> Strange splendour and strange gloom
> Alike confuse the path
> Of customary faith. . . .
>
> (*Po*, 400)

Other statements appall in any generation:

> Ho, ye
> Who loved our Flag
> Only because there flapp'd none other rag
> Which gentlemen might doff to, and such be,
> 'Save your gentility!
> For leagued, alas, are we
> With many a faithful rogue
> Discrediting bright Truth with dirt and brogue.
>
> (*Po*, 400–401)

(Emily's letter already quoted adds: "There are two lines in one Ode that I could wish were not there [the last two above]. If I have said anything presumptuous, please forgive it."[10] Yet, this violent poem moves to a quietly triumphal close through a paean to "the light store / And daisied path / Of Poverty" (*Po*, 399–402).

"Sponsa Dei" (ode 5) begins with apparent paradox:

> What is this Maiden fair,
> The laughing of whose eye
> Is in man's heart renew'd virginity;
> Who yet sick longing breeds
> For marriage which exceeds
> The inventive guess of Love to satisfy
>
> (*Po*, 403)

but soon relinquishes the courtly lover's accent for the explicit self-answering question which is his stated general theme:

> What if this Lady be thy Soul, and He
> Who claims to enjoy her sacred beauty be,
> Not thou, but God. . . .
>
> (*Po*, 404)

"Legem Tuam Dilexi" (ode 6) is as powerful as the preceding poem is delicate. Dealing on one level with religious vows freely taken,

Patmore considers, with some remarkable images, several aspects of law and restraint countering or supporting in the natural/supernatural order in which he chooses to situate himself. It should be remembered that at the time of writing, Patmore's beloved daughter had recently made her religious profession, and the second marriage, which we have reason to believe was unconsummated, was wearing to its close in Mary Patmore's death. Patmore would not have used the term "sublimation" but it does suggest itself. The opening lines arrest attention:

> The "Infinite." Word horrible! at feud
> With life, and the braced mood
> Of power and joy and love.
>
> *(Po,* 405)

A little later,

> But for compulsion of strong grace,
> The pebble in the road
> Would straight explode,
> And fill the ghastly boundlessness of space.
>
> *(Po,* 405)

The classic lines are midmost:

> . . . Man,
> Darling of God, . . .
> . . . Who woos his will
> To wedlock with His own, and does distil
> To that drop's span
> The attar of all rose-fields of all love![11]
>
> *(Po,* 406)

This makes sense of the soul's "bonds unbid," the vows of religion. Patmore disposes glibly of poverty and obedience but is eloquent on chastity, "bartering life's dear bliss for pain." An impressive passage enlarges upon this:

> For joy (rejoice ye Few that tasted have!)
> Is Love's obedience
> Against the genial laws of natural sense,
> Whose wide, self-dissipating wave,
> Prison'd in artful dykes,
> Trembling returns and strikes
> Thence to its source again,
> In backward billows fleet,

> Crest crossing crest ecstatic as they greet,
> Thrilling each vein,
> Exploring every chasm and cove
> Of the full heart with floods of honied love,
> And every principal street
> And obscure alley and lane
> Of the intricate brain
> With brimming rivers of light and breezes sweet
> Of the primordial heat. . . .
>
> (*Po*, 407–408)

Finally, the "intense life" is either "Lost" or in some way distorted—"ludicrously display'd"—by ambiguous "distance" or misunderstanding, "as a soaring eagle, or a horse . . . May seem a gust-driv'n rag or a dead stone." With a pearls-before-swine gesture Patmore leaves off his explanation:

> Fitly revering the Wild Ass's bray,
> Also his hoof,
> Of which . . . the marks remain
> Where the religious walls have hid the bright reproof. . .
>
> (*Po*, 408)

presumably post-Reformation despoiling of monasteries and recent echoes of the same, stirred by the mid-century restoration of the Roman Catholic hierarchy in England and the resurgence of religious congregations like that to which his daughter belonged, whose foundress had under extraordinary circumstances renounced her marriage.[12] Doubtless both Emily and Mary Patmore were on his mind, and Patmore's own strain until the third marriage was possible may have had something to do with his cantankerous creativity.

Ode 7, "To the Body," is Patmore's most forthrightly physical yet delicately successful Incarnation-Resurrection-virginity poem. After the brief blazon (the first two lines of which he accuses Swinburne of plagiarizing),[13]

> Little, sequester'd pleasure-house
> For God and for His Spouse;
> Elaborately, yea, past conceiving, fair,
> Since, from the graced decorum of the hair,
> Ev'n to the tingling, sweet
> Soles of the simple, earth-confiding feet,
> And from the inmost heart
> Outward unto the thin

> Silk curtains of the skin,
> Every least part
> Astonish'd hears
> And sweet replies to some like region of the spheres. . .
>
> (*Po*, 408–409)

the poet adverts to the human condition which includes death for a
time but glory soon after. He concludes:

> O, if the pleasures I have known in thee
> But my poor faith's poor first-fruits be,
> What quintessential, keen, ethereal bliss
> Then shall be his
> Who has thy birth-time's consecrating dew
> For death's sweet chrism retain'd,
> Quick, tender, virginal, and unprofaned!
>
> (*Po*, 410)

In ode 8, "'Sing Us One of the Songs of Sion,'" the strange land to
which England is likened (by its Exodus imagery—Aaron, Pharaoh,
flies, frogs) is Egypt rather than Babylon. The true leader of the
Chosen, according to Connolly's gloss, is Newman, whom Patmore
aspires to imitate by dealing "fair Sion's foolish foes / Such blows!"
(*Po*, 411). "Deliciae Sapientiae de Amore" (ode 9) again sets the
speaker "a beggar by the Porch / Of the glad Palace of Virginity"
where those who follow the Lamb are seen as in the Book of Revela-
tion. It is too heavily populated to suggest mystical rapture, and full of
dogmatic statements such as: "the Elect . . . affect / Nothing but
God" either mediately, through conjugal love, or directly, through
virginity—"Or mediate or direct, / Nothing but God, / The Husband
of the Heavens . . ." (*Po*, 411, 415–16). Patmore tells Harriet Robson
he wrote this poem in two hours.[14] It is one of the original nine odes
and could be considered a worksheet toward the projected *Marriage
of the Blessed Virgin*. Ode 10, "The Cry at Midnight"—"'Our bridegroom's near'" is an elitist pleasantry:

> Who judge of Plays from their own penny gaff,
> At God's great theatre will hiss and laugh;
> For what's a Saint to them
> Brought up in modern virtues brummagem?
>
> (*Po*, 416)

"Auras of Delight" (ode 11) warns against presumptuousness and
delusion in complex dove-snake imagery.

The Psyche odes, "Eros and Psyche" (12), "De Natura Deorum" (13), and "Psyche's Discontent" (14) are important efforts in spiritual psychology. They are dialogues, with a certain lightness which some (Hopkins, for instance) have found disconcerting, but their basic fidelity to the experience of a soul desirous of giving itself wholly to God comes through in the classical myth most apt for Patmore's theme. Their apparent extravagance pales beside the language of the spiritual classics Patmore implicitly invokes—the lushness of the *Exercises of St. Gertrude*, the playfulness and homeliness of Julian of Norwich, the ardors of saints John of the Cross and Teresa of Avila, and of course the oriental imagery and eloquence of parts of Sacred Scripture. Such writings try to translate into human terms the reality of God wooing the soul and the soul seeking to respond, at first hampered by limited vision and by fear of the cost, then surrendering to the strong attraction and overwhelmed by the joy of union, yet subject still to lapses and vicissitudes and growth in the relationship. The Psyche odes are best approached with prior reading of Patmore to brace one for the combination of intensity, coyness, precept, preposterousness, and spiritual insight.

Four more odes complete the second book of the *Unknown Eros*. "Pain" (15), purifying and not morbid, is personified as a lover but ultimately dealt with by "the learned spirit" who "knows both how to have thee and to lack" (*Po*, 436). "Prophets Who Cannot Sing" (16) upholds the "people of a harsh and stammering tongue" who utter not the sweet songs of natural beauty but ineffable tidings of "unveil'd heavens,"

> Praise that in chiming numbers will not run;
> At least from David until Dante, none
> And none since him.
>
> *(Po, 437)*

"The Child's Purchase" (17), originally meant to introduce the *Marriage of the Blessed Virgin*, is a long self-contained poem opening with a parable of a child who gives back his gift-coin for a kiss—so the poet gives his "golden speech" back to his "Mother and God's." Then a litany of ten- to fifteen-line invocations ending with "Ora pro me" brings together a wealth of scriptural and liturgical imagery along with a measure of Psyche-like description that is not always sublime or even felicitous: "Sunshiny Peak of human personality"; "Bright Blush, that sav'st our shame from shamelessness" (*Po*, 441). There are firmer conceits and traces of the old narrative skill: "Our only Saviour from an abstract Christ" (*Po*, 442); "Prism whereby / Alone we see /

Heav'n's light in its triplicity" (*Po*, 440); ". . . holding a little thy soft breath, / Thou underwent'st the ceremony of death" (*Po*, 443). The ode ends with something like a Chaucerian retractation:

> Bless thou the work
> Which, done, redeems my many wasted days,
> Makes white the murk,
> And crowns the few which thou wilt not dispraise.
>
> (*Po*, 443)

But the last word is "Dead Language" (ode 18). Reproached for speaking truth's own scorn and tenderness rather than cloaking his thoughts more acceptably, the poet is not daunted by the prospect of "acorn-munchers" rending him "limb from limb" but says no one pays any attention to him—"is not mine a language dead?" Patmore's signing off as rejected prophet and not as Marian bard indicates the prevailing mood of his later days without blocking out the strange variety in this last spate of poems.[15]

CHAPTER 6

Patmore's Women

I *The Wives*

A SSIGNING identity to Patmore heroines contributes little to our understanding of the poems, although it enhances the poems' contribution to the biography. Emily Augusta Patmore herself starts us off with a letter evidently written in 1853: "Coventry's new book of poetry [*Tamerton Church-Tower*] is just come out . . . [the omissions are Champneys's]. There is a long poem called 'Honoria' addressed to me. There is also a lady named 'Blanche' who is taken from R—, not in mind but in person merely. It is exactly like her. . . ."[1] "R—," Champneys tells us, is a niece of Emily's. A mysterious pair of entries in Patmore's hand: "R.R.C." and "E.A.P.," the latter his wife's initials, can be clearly made out beneath a less legible "'Thou hast redeemed the red' etc."[2] in the margin of Patmore's copy, heavily annotated (after his conversion to Catholicism), of the two-volume descriptive index to Swedenborg's *Arcana Coelestia*.[3]

We escape the futility of judging or too definitely categorizing Patmore's women themselves by taking at face value his distinction between right and wrong ways of loving them. The contrasting personalities (rather than characters) of Blanche and Ruth in "Tamerton Church-Tower" do suggest yieldingness and reserve, but the focus is on the young man's expectations. Patmore's loves and fictions—they are in general and ideal terms much related and all virtuous—include both the stately (his first and second wives; Ruth in "Tamerton Church-Tower"; Honoria in the *Angel*; Alice Meynell) and the childlike (his third wife; Blanche in "Tamerton Church-Tower"; Amelia, the heroine of the title poem of the 1878 collection; Psyche of the odes; Jane in the *Victories of Love*). There is considerable blurring, of course, in real life and in the poems. Harriet Patmore is a latter-day Honoria,[4] and the dominant wife-as-child motif in the preludes to the cantos of the *Angel*, books 1 and 2, is elaborated beyond the demands of Victorian social history, legal custom or literary convention.

One of the readiest examples of blending or superimposing is Patmore's own favorite,[5] his "little idyll," "Amelia," which is metrically but not really chronologically a bridge between the *Angel* and the odes. J. C. Reid's comment on it is very apt: "One of the reasons why *Amelia* is such a typically Patmorean poem is that to make a success of a piece in which a middle-aged lover takes his young fiancée to the grave of her predecessor requires unusual purity and innocence of spirit."[6] Reid follows Champneys in giving Patmore's first wife as first reference for this poem: "Amelia" is a form of "Emily"; "With great, kind eyes, in whose brown shade / Bright Venus and her Baby play'd" describes Emily; it was to Hastings, "the little, bright, surf-breathing town," that Patmore had taken Emily on their honeymoon. (Blanche drowned at Edgcumb was brown-eyed too.) But the poem is at least partly Harriet's. Consider the following points: the stated age difference; the role of successor to a deceased former love; the "baby" manner, which Emily Honoria's travel diary had noted as characteristic of Miss Robson several years before (both Emily Augusta and Mary Patmore were mature and dignified to a degree remarked in others' reminiscence of them); the seaside town of Hastings where the Patmores lived from 1875 until ten years after the third marriage and where Harriet was often with them; the note of patient waiting with ultimate possession assured (Patmore married Harriet in 1881, a year and a half after Mary's death); the possibility, unique to Harriet, of a mother who was apprehensive about the relationship between her daughter and an older man. This is not to suggest that there was on Patmore's part any infidelity to his second wife; nor was there any to his third wife during the few years at the end of his life when he worshipped Alice Meynell. Coventry Patmore was simply so constituted by temperament and so bolstered by theory that he could be actually and happily married to one woman while ideally and lyrically in love with another. With both Harriet and Alice, Patmore talks and corresponds at length about poetry and intellectual matters. Frederick Page in a letter of 18 December 1935, taking Derek Patmore to task for implying that Coventry was not above reproach in his attitude toward either lady, mentions "letters written in the '70's . . . to Harriet Robson" which dealt "with such subjects as the metre of the odes, and the proposed poem on the Marriage of the Virgin, on sacred music, on Swedenborg, on Schopenhauer, on Goethe." These letters, or rather extracts from letters, are what Champneys quotes copiously[7] and identifies as "written between 1873 and 1878 to an intimate and sympathetic friend." They "throw much light upon the circumstances, physical and mental, under which the later Odes were written. . . ." Writing to Emily Honoria's biographer (about 1925) Champneys confirms that the "intimate and sympathetic friend" is Harriet and places her in a good light:

The second wife, whom I knew well, was a real and most unselfish saint, though her qualities were revealed only to a few. Patmore's transcendental development owes much to her; though she was not fully alive to his artistic merits.

His widow was a member of the home circle for many years—she and Mary Patmore were the closest and most intimate friends—and she had the deepest appreciation of his poetry both in subject and form. It was to her . . . that all those remarkable letters were written which give so vivid a psychological insight into the mind of the poet in the throes of creation. . . . It was a real pleasure to me to gather . . . that you seemed to have appreciated her thoroughly. She was and is most worthy of it, but her quality is not patent to all and the bitterness she had to endure in the latest years was nobly borne; and all, I thank God, came right at the last.

. . . I shall hope in all events to preserve my respect for Mrs. Meynell, and my reverence for Patmore will never be abated.[8]

Champneys goes on to deplore a "jewel transaction"—Coventry had long loved and collected jewels, partly perhaps as a good investment, and during their brief friendship delighted in having Alice Meynell wear them. Some gift Coventry pressed upon Alice appeared to Champneys out of order, and he went so far as to blame Mrs. Meynell for the subsequent "impoverishment" of Patmore's widow.

II   *Alice Meynell*

Frederick Page defends both Patmore and Alice Meynell with gallantry and conviction. Viola Meynell's memoir of her mother deals beautifully with the meteoric friendship, and without adverting to anxiety quotes letters which would certainly allay any apprehension. The literary correspondence is represented by Alice's praise of Coventry's poems and forthright criticism of some of the essays he had gathered into *Principle in Art*. She destroyed most of his letters to her, but several from Coventry to her husband are frank and to the point. Alice writes to Coventry:

I have never told you what I think of your poetry. It is the greatest thing in the world, the most harrowing and the sweetest. I can hardly realise that he who has written it and who is greater than his words is celestially kind to me and calls me friend.[9]

I would ask you to reconsider *Distinction*. Believe me, it does such injustice to living writers (so does *William Barnes* indeed) that it is almost a confession that you do not thoroughly know the men you slight. And that is so extremely irritating to people that I am inclined to think it has caused the partial boycotting of your work.

But worse than this is the quarrel in it with the *Spectator* and the *Guardian*. Your attitude has been always one of singular dignity. . . . Nor does *Distinction* contain anything that does not appear in one form or another elsewhere.[10]

To Wilfrid Meynell Coventry writes from Lymington:

Your wife is leaving us this afternoon, and I feel that I have been done out of at least half my expected fortnight. Best part of three days' absence in London, and three days more during which she was invisible, except at meals, slaving at pot-boilers! I feel too savage to thank you as I should for the remaining week.[11]

Alice herself writes home during the same visit:

Thank you, dearest Love, for your letter. . . . If you suppose I am not thinking of your darlingness at work through the weary day, you are much mistaken. Coventry is so melancholy at my working that I am glad that the Kipling is over, though I enjoyed doing it. We have been for a most exquisite drive, and all the way I thought of my beloved boy sitting beside the fender.[12]

The Meynell children shared the friendship as the following note testifies, and in later life recalled somewhat formidable dinners at either home when Piffie toed the mark and the grown-up Tennyson teased cats and little girls:[13] "My own girl,—I hope you had a nice journey and warm feet and a better head. You're a lovely woman. Tell Mr. Patmore he's a brick for loving you so much, and that I appreciate him awfully. Viola's in perfect spirits now. Miss Swain says I've been an eccelentissima figlia!"[14] Viola describes Patmore's visits, each a "stirring event," his "quality of rarity," and "the importance that was his naturally." When in London, "he shared a little in my parents' social life, even as he liked to share their working life, though to one so fastidious as he none but the choicest occasions might be offered." The visits however stopped, the demanding Patmore somehow made to realize the need to draw back. He took hard Mrs. Meynell's new friendship with George Meredith, writing to Wilfrid to decline an opportunity to work with her again:

It may seem absurd to you and herself, but my power of doing anything more in that or any other matter has been paralyzed by my finding, from her own words and acts, that my primacy in her friendship has been superseded. I shall be as much pleased as I can be at anything by appearing in her new Anthology, and, as I get no news from her now, I shall be grateful for anything you can tell me about her.[15]

The woman who was worshipped by such diverse literary men as Francis Thompson, Coventry Patmore, and George Meredith maintained with each a relationship of delicate graciousness which they might not transgress. That her reserve was sometimes unintended coldness touched Patmore the most deeply as the explorer of spiritually nuanced affectivity in terms both sponsal and transcendent. Alice Meynell's own inadequacy is gently pointed to in her daughter's memoir and sadly acknowledged by Alice herself to the same nun to whom Champneys wrote during her work on Patmore's daughter's biography:

She was selfless, compassionate, and, one would have said, was made of love, but she could fail to satisfy the friends she loved most, him above any other. And that this particular kind of failure formed a definite feature of her life is clearly recognized in a letter written by her in her latest years. . . . to a nun of extraordinary holiness and intelligence, to whom my mother turned for wisdom and to whom she broke unhappy silences. "All my troubles . . . are little, old, foolish, trivial, as they always were. . . . But as to sorrow, my failure of love to those that loved me can never be cancelled or undone. . . ." Probably . . . she was so provided with love within her family . . . that she did not make those who loved her feel her need of them.[16]

The importance of these women—the three wives and Alice Meynell—in Coventry Patmore's personal and creative life cannot be overestimated. His major preoccupation with marriage and its analogues—he constantly uses the analogy of sex, especially in his poetry and in the aphorisms which make up *The Rod, the Root, and the Flower*—and his fascination with virginity and with relationships transcending physical marriage are ultimately translatable into his understanding of the relationship of the soul to God. Yet where he is most explicit and at the same time most intentionally "mystical" in *The Rod, the Root, and the Flower*, he reiterates again and again the

legitimacy and necessity of return to the delights of the senses after a
period of renunciation or of purely spiritual contemplation.

After the main dogmas, which are of faith, the teaching of theologians is very
largely derived from facts of psychology within the reach of everyone who
chooses to pay the cost. For example . . . there are four states or aspects of
the Soul. . . . The Morning is the mood of glad, free, and hopeful worship,
supplication, and thanksgiving; the Noon is the perfect state of contemplation or spiritual fruition; this cannot be sustained . . . for very long, and it
passes into the "Evening joy," in which the Soul turns, not from God, but to
God in His creatures—to all natural delights, rendered natural indeed by
supernatural insight. Lastly, Night is that condition of the Soul which . . .
occupies by far the greatest part of the lives even of the most holy, but which
will have no existence when the remains of corruption which cause the
darkness shall have passed away.[17]

In passages like this, as in his seizing upon "heavenly marriage"
statements in Swedenborg, one feels that Patmore is building up
theoretical justification for his intuition and experience. His prose
often staggers under this burden, and his verse is sometimes over-
weighted with argument (especially the preludes to the cantos of the
Angel), but he generally carries it off, as an open-minded reader of the
Angel and the odes will concede. Such a reader is assisted by
forewarning of Patmore's conscious idealization of sex and by recognition of the strong biographical thread running through his work. Not
much attention has been paid to the alternation of fulfillment and
denial in Patmore's life during the successive ascendencies of Emily
Augusta, Mary, Harriet, and Alice Meynell. The perfect first marriage is the given from which Patmore develops his theme. Emily,
knowing her death was near, urged remarriage, writing propheti-
cally, "your dear wife, whom you will love as a friend, will soon learn
that her best way of expressing her love for you will be to watch
tenderly over your little lambs. . . . I have brought the children to
look forward to your second marriage as a probable and desirable
thing."[18] Whatever she meant by "love as a friend" she seems to have
described her actual successor whose devotion to Emily's children
was exemplary even if at times oversolicitous[19] and who, according to
a solitary but reliable authority (Emily Honoria's biographer, who
was a friend of Bertha and Harriet Patmore and of the Meynells as
well as of Champneys), during her marriage to Patmore continued to
live in conformity with a vow of virginity she had made.[20]

Champneys and Derek Patmore after him simply refer to Patmore's "Autobiography"[21] where he speaks of being daunted by Miss

Byles's "formal religious promise never to marry" until he discovered "how easily such undertakings are dispensed with in the Catholic Church." J. C. Reid quarrels with "L. Wheaton's" assertion that Mary Patmore kept her private vow because he considers an unconsummated marriage un-Catholic and inconceivable for Coventry. But Reid is at some disadvantage in not knowing the origin of the Wheaton article (its author Reid supposes to depend on Champneys whose words "he has misunderstood") and in being unfamiliar with sufficient precedent for such a marriage. Reid does, however, allow for an impediment to normal marriage relations in the "later chronic invalidism" of the second wife, and recognizes "Patmore's struggle [particularly in the Psyche odes] . . . to achieve a sublimation of the sensual in the spiritual."[22] Reid's handling of the third marriage is (except for an occasional minor inaccuracy like calling Harriet Robson a school fellow of the poet's eldest daughter)[23] sensitive and thoroughly consistent with what is verifiable.

What is curious, in the same quasi-prophetic vein as the early poetic dwelling on the death of a young wife, is the role of Mary Churchill who, in book 2 of the *Victories of Love* (1862)—the fourth and last completed book of the projected six-part *Angel*—is represented as having chosen to remain single for religious reasons. Her "worldly" sister, Lady Clitheroe, appeals to Frederick's mother, Mrs. Graham:

> Do, dear Aunt, use your influence,
> And try to teach some plain good sense
> To Mary. 'Tis not yet too late
> To make her change her chosen state
> Of single silliness. In truth
> I fancy that, with fading youth,
> Her will now wavers. . . .
> This marrying of Nieces daunts
> The bravest souls of maiden Aunts.
> . . . .
> She twice refused George Vane, you know;
> Yet, when he died three years ago
> In the Indian War, she put on gray,
> And wears no colours to this day.

(Po, 304)

Mary herself writes to her clergyman father:

> Charles does me honour, but 'twere vain
> To reconsider now again,

And so to doubt the clear-shown truth
I sought for, and received, when youth,
Being fair, and woo'd by one whose love
Was lovely, fail'd my mind to move.
.   .   .   .   .   .   :   .   .   .   .   .

I grieve for my infirmity,
And ignorance of how to be
Faithful, at once, to the heavenly life,
And the fond duties of a wife.
Narrow am I and want the art
To love two things with all my heart.

(*Po*, 306)

Patmore was not to meet, convince, and marry his reluctant Mary until 1864. Nor would he really have to try to understand consecrated virginity until his daughter Emily asked to become a nun eight years later. Frederick Page's hypothesis[24] that several of the odes were meant to be parts of the sequel to the *Victories of Love* in the full scheme of a six-book *Angel* suggests that Frederick Graham followed the dying Jane's recommendation to remarry by taking Mary Churchill as his second wife. Some odes—"Tired Memory," "The Azalea," "The Toys," "Departure," "If I Were Dead"—do sit more comfortably as spoken by the fictional Frederick than simply as adapted autobiography. The slight but needed distance so achieved is satisfying enough to make us wonder why Page's idea has not gained more currency. Reid, for instance, finds "parts of Mr. Page's argument . . . strained,"[25] and objects that "the group of widower's poems is so much more personal than anything in his previous work that Patmore must have felt . . . it . . . a kind of desecration to allot to fictitious characters utterances so immediately struck from his own poignant experience."[26] One could reply with equal conviction that to use such intense experience at all Patmore the artist would have welcomed and even required a mask.

CHAPTER 7

Prosody and Later Prose

I Prosodic Theory

WHETHER or not one shares Frederick Page's perception of a line of development from which the seemingly irregular and often sublime odes could have issued prosodically and thematically from the filled-out, basically realistic quatrains of the *Angel in the House* and couplets of the *Victories of Love*, Patmore's continual rearranging suggests both that he saw his work as a whole and that he kept getting better ideas about it. Dropped poems and early versions are treated as if they did not exist, and what Patmore presented in final form in 1886 he meant to supersede his offerings of 1844, 1853, 1854–1856, 1878, etc.—thus he stated in the preface to the 1886 and subsequent editions of his *Poems*, that

> With this reprint I believe that I am closing my task as a poet, having traversed the ground and reached the end which, in my youth, I saw before me. I have written little, but it is all my best; I have never spoken when I had nothing to say, nor spared time or labour to make my words true. I have respected posterity; and should there be a posterity which cares for letters, I dare to hope that it will respect me.

With the Patmore canon before us in a single volume—we speak only of the poetry—arranged chronologically by first publication (but with complete fidelity to Patmore's final inclusions and revisions) it is easy to see that there is no discontinuity. There is growth between 1844 and the finished *Angel*, but after the coming of age in 1854 with the *Betrothal* (first part of the *Angel*) the touch is sure and the experience successfully transmuted. The poems illustrate the "seemingly unconscious *finish from within*" he finds so rare.[1] The step from *Angel* to *Eros* is not as great as critics contemporary with Patmore would have us believe. The obvious differences include the absence of a sustaining narrative thread (although the widower odes provide a tenuous one) and an apparently free shape on the page. The metrical configuration of the later poems according to Patmore's principles enhances the delicate precision of the diction and imagery, and whether or not he had tired of the facile regularity of the earlier work as Reid suggests,[2] he later rounded out his theorizing by practice with the "iambic ode, erroneously called 'irregular,' . . . a tetrameter with almost unlimited liberty of catalexis, to suit the variations of the high and stately lyrical feeling which can alone justify the use of this measure."[3]

Lest anyone be put off by the term "practice" for such finished products, we have the poet's own statement to Mackenzie Bell in a letter of 17 January 1894:[4] "When I spoke in the 'Fortnightly,' of having been engaged for ten years in recommending that metre, I meant that I had done so by supplying illustrations of its use in my Poem called the 'Unknown Eros' & in other pieces." The *Fortnightly* article referred to, "Francis Thompson, a New Poet," is one of those collected in *Courage in Politics*; this article is very faithful to the pronouncements and even to the expression of the "Essay on English Metrical Law" which first appeared as a review article in the *North British Review* in 1857[5] and was reprinted, slightly modified, with *Amelia* in 1878, and at the end of the two-volume collected edition of Patmore's *Poems* from 1886 on. The Thompson essay recalls the years between 1867 and 1877 as the period which Patmore devoted mainly to demonstrating "the capacities of the iambic tetrameter with unlimited catalexis, which is commonly called the 'irregular' ode, though it is really as 'regular' as any other English metre . . . if its subtle laws are truly considered and obeyed."[6] A tetrameter for Patmore is four dipodes or eight feet (see below, p. 110). By catalexis Patmore means using fewer syllables than a normal line would require, while retaining the normal line's time value because the omissions correspond to rests in a musical measure. His rationale is clear, faithful as description and reasonable as justification of how and when the poet playing by ear falls into the apparently free iambics of *Amelia* and the *Unknown Eros*.

Patmore's study, for all George Saintsbury's objection that it "simply swarms with crotchety and temerarious deliverances,"[7] has the great merit of good sense and applicability—Saintsbury, eminent historian of criticism and of prosody, does allow Patmore "a knowledge, almost unique for his time, of the actual history of his subject; freedom from many popular errors, a true sense of poetry, and a large number of acute and valuable aperçus." A prosodist a generation later claims that Patmore's fellow poets and theorizers "found in the essay the first intelligent attempt to solve a problem which interested them all—how to include within the principles of English versification the peculiarities of the newly recovered body of Old English poetry."[8] Further, "Hopkins' sprung rhythm, and for that matter most of his running rhythm, follows Patmore's theories almost to the letter"; Patmore's "use of a musical scansion-notation between bar lines is precisely what Hopkins needed to convey his metrical intentions," although "Patmore and Hopkins never saw how they complemented each other."[9] In fact, Hopkins takes issue with several points in Patmore's essay.[10] William Henry Gardner calls attention to Patmore's own use of sprung rhythm in "Wind and Wave," although the *Essay on English Metrical Law* in its preoccupation with time does not specifically advert to the rhythmic effect so natural to Hopkins and so readily described in terms of juxtaposed stress.

Hopkins's appreciation of Patmore as a poet comes through strongly in letters to Robert Bridges who does not entirely share it—"By the by how can you speak of Patmore as you do? I read his *Unknown Eros* well before leaving Oxford. He shows a mastery of phrase, of the rhetoric of verse, which belongs to the tradition of Shakespeare and Milton and in which you could not find him a living equal. . . ."[11] The Hopkins-Patmore correspondence is as vital an exchange as can be found between poets who think so much alike and sound so different. They actually met and talked together only a few times, each maintaining a fascinated independence. Their letters deal as much with literary matters external to both as with Hopkins's suggestions (through the fall and early winter of 1883–1884, at Patmore's request soon after they had first met) about the forthcoming revised edition of *Poems by Coventry Patmore* (1886). This correspondence dispels the legend begun by Patmore himself and passed on unexamined, that Hopkins told Patmore to burn his quintessential prose treatise *Sponsa Dei* (which almost certainly survives in spirit and in unassembled fragments in the later essays and aphorisms). "Milltown, Dublin, May 6, 1888. My dear Mr. Patmore, Your news was that you had burnt the book called 'Sponsa Dei,' and that on reflexion upon remarks of mine. I wish I had been more guarded in making them. . . . My objections were not final: they were but considerations (I forget now, with one exception, what they were). . . ."[12] The "remarks" remain a mystery.

Patmore had no disciples—Francis Thompson came late and briefly under his influence; Hopkins had no master—Bridges and Dixon were friends and sounding boards but not mentors. The relationship between Patmore and Hopkins was significant to each but of a very few years' duration, beginning only in 1883 and cut off by the death of the younger man in 1889. Patmore's letter to Bridges on this occasion (12 August 1889) makes no reference to Hopkins's poems. Patmore had asked to see them in 1884, but was nonplussed by their "altogether unprecedented system of alliteration and compound words."[13]

I can well understand how terrible a loss you have suffered in the death of Gerard Hopkins—you who saw so much more of him than I did. I spent three days with him at Stonyhurst, and he stayed a week with me here; and that, with the exception of a somewhat abundant correspondence by letter, is all the communication I had with him; but this was enough to awaken in me a reverence and affection, the like of which I have never felt for any other man but one, that one being Frederick Greenwood. . . . Gerard Hopkins was the only orthodox, and as far as I could see, saintly man in whom religion had absolutely no narrowing effect upon his general opinions and sympathies. . . . The *authority* of his goodness was so great with me that I threw the manuscript of a little book [*Sponsa Dei*] . . . into the fire, simply because, when he had read it, he said with a grave look, "That's telling secrets." This little book had been the work of ten years' continual meditations, and could not but have made a greater effect than all the rest I have ever written; but his doubt was final with me.

I am very glad that you are to write a memorial of him. It is quite right that it should be privately printed. I as one of his friends, should protest against any attempt to share him with the public, to whom little of what was most truly characteristic in him could be communicated.[14]

A fair amount of the Hopkins-Patmore correspondence concerns language and prosody. Hopkins urges the naturalness of old English stress patterns and sprung rhythm, citing nursery rhymes and weather saws as irrefutable examples. Patmore is increasingly interested in time as measure—he had made up his mind on the subject as early as 1857.

Sidney Colvin calls Patmore's essay on English meters "the most luminous thing that has been written on that puzzling subject."[15] but Patmore gives credit to an eighteenth-century metrist for the initial breakthrough: "Joshuah Steele has . . . propounded . . . the true view of metre, as being primarily based upon isochronous divisions by ictuses or accents; and he . . . clearly declared the necessity of measuring pauses. . . ."[16] Steele had seen that it was not enough to consider the two elements of accent and quantity when there were really five at play in verse rhythm: "accent, emphasis, quantity, pause, force,"[17] and he made what was for Patmore a key statement on the use of pause:

> Our language which (to speak according to the Greek prosody) abounds with *iambics, trochees, spondees, dactyls,* and *anapaests,* makes agreeable *hexameters* with five cadences of words, and the quantity of one more left for pauses.
> But the precise number of ten syllables are not always the necessary complement of the five cadences of words; for if there are dactyllic feet, the number of syllables may be increased without any injury to the measure.[18]

The native flexibility of English verse resides then in the temporal rhythm which depends on the variously filled but equally long intervals marked by a "time beater . . . [which] for the most part . . . *has no material or external existence at all,* but has its place in the mind, which craves measure in everything."[19] Patmore has assumed our agreement that "Metre, in the primary degree of a simple series of isochronous intervals, marked by accents, is as natural to spoken language as an even pace is natural to walking."[20] The intervals are filled with syllables or silence; the marker or time beater is "accent." Hopkins in some exasperation writes: "The ictus of our verse is founded on and in the beginning the very same as the stress which is our accent. . . . You ought . . . to say once clearly what English accent is and is not."[21]

Patmore does in fact say a lot about accent. It includes ictus and tone (acute, or high, and, when rhetoric requires, grave), and admits loudness as an element. But "elevation of tone and ictus have no *necessary* association with long quantity," and "a permanent tone dwelling on certain words would render poetry and song impossible. . . . The compound change of tone, called the 'circumflex' accent, is . . . as liable to commence with a fall as with a rise."[22] It is then less than true that "Patmore had not distinguished spoken accent from *ictus* or metrical accent."[23] The latter he most prudently defines by function rather than by enumeration of its possible ingredients. It is simply that which measures equal intervals of time and is *"itself unmeasured"*—this "'ictus' or 'beat,' actual or mental, . . . like a post in a chain railing, shall mark the end of one space, and the commencement of another."[24] On the subject of time (in recognizing isochronous intervals) Patmore provides an important clarification with a helpful example:

The time occupied in the actual articulation of a syllable is not necessarily its metrical value. *The time of a syllable in combination, is that which elapses from its commencement to the commencement of the succeeding syllable:* so that the monosyllables, a, as, ask, asks, ask'st, though requiring five degrees of time for their articulation, may have precisely the same temporal value in verse, just as, in music played *staccato* on the pianoforte, the actual duration of sound in a crotchet or a quaver note may be the same, the metrical value depending altogether on the difference of the time which elapses before the commencement of the succeeding note.[25]

Characteristically Patmore believes that "language should always seem to *feel*, though not to *suffer from* the bonds of verse" and reminds us that art "must have a body as well as a soul." Early in the essay comes this wishful self-portrait:

The best poet is . . . he whose language combines the greatest imaginative accuracy with the most elaborate and sensible metrical organization, and who in his verse, preserves everywhere the living sense of metre, not so much by unvarying obedience to, as by innumerable small departures from, its *modulus*.[26]

(That this should describe Hopkins as well as himself would not have occurred to Patmore.)

Having established his general principle of evenly timed metrical units which can include silent intervals (anywhere, not just at the end of a line), Patmore enunciates his less obvious law that the real integer of English verse is the dipode, "the space which is bounded by *alternate* accents," or two feet in most other metrists' parlance. "All English verses in common cadence are therefore dimeters, trimeters, or tetrameters, and consist, when they are *full*, i.e., without *catalexis*, of eight, twelve or sixteen syllables."[27] Patmore is on home ground in discussing the octosyllabic couplet and quatrain, "two of the most important measures we have," and settles to his own satisfaction the age-long dispute about rhyme—"The metrical function of rhyme, like that of alliteration, has never yet been fully recognized."[28] The authority both of his predecessors and of his own ear (which Osbert Burdett believed faulty and in need of the discipline afforded by Patmore's early use of simple measures)[29] assures him that rhyme is "the highest metrical power we have" and that "it is almost impossible, by even the most skilful arrangement of unrhymed verses, to produce a recurrent metre of several lines long."[30]

Is it subtlety or willfulness which prompts him to distinguish the "true Alexandrine" (a tetrameter with "a middle and a final pause each equal to a foot") from the "so-called 'Alexandrine' at the end of the Spenserian stanza" (which, because it generally lacks a middle pause, must be "the mere filling up of the trimeter")?[31] Of the same lineage as the true or tetrameter Alexandrine are the ballad meter of fourteen syllables or "the stave of 'eight and six'" ("properly managed there is no other metre so well able to represent the combined dignity and impetuosity of the heroic hexameter") and the full or acatalectic tetrameter of sixteen syllables (plain octosyllabics, paired as couplets or half-quatrains). Notice how Patmore has covered his own entire practice—the fourteeners of the 1844 *Poems* and *Tamerton Church-Tower*, the octosyllabic quatrains of the *Angel in the House* and couplets of the *Victories of Love*, the catalectic measure of *Amelia* and the odes.

Blank verse he is happy to leave to Milton. It is very taxing, having "little or no rhythm of its own," and requires the poet "to create the rhythm as he writes"—

But the great difficulty, as well as delight, of this measure is not in variety of pause, tone, and stress, for its own sake. Such variety must be incessantly inspired by, and expressive of, ever-varying emotion. Every alteration of the position of the grammatical pause, every deviation from the strict and dull iambic rhythm, must be either sense or nonsense. *Such change is as real a mode of expressing emotion as words themselves are of expressing thought;* and when the means exist without reference to their proper ends, the effect of the 'variety' thereby obtained, is more offensive to a right judgment, than the dulness which is supposed to be avoided.[32]

One reason for Patmore's discomfort with blank verse is that it foregoes rhyme. The following is revealing: in blank verse "the lines should always be catalectic, since, in the absence of rhyme a measurable final pause is the only means of marking the separate existence of the verses. . . ."[33]

Patmore has some good things to say about Chaucer's rhyme royal or "rhythm royal" as the essay calls it, fewer about the "Pope couplet," none about the sonnet (which after his earliest period he never used himself—of the three in the 1844 volume only one was retained in 1853 and this vanished by 1878). Throughout his reluctant discussion he avoids naming ten-syllable lines pentameters.

But in the world he sees through the spectacles of his own tetrameters Patmore exercises an easy sway, convinced all along that "the musical and metrical expression of emotion is an instinct, and not an artifice."[34] Years later C. S. Lewis gives striking testimony to the sureness of Patmore's instinct: "I have just finished *The Angel in the House*. Amazing poet! How all of a piece it is—how the rivetted metre both exposes and illustrates his almost fanatical love of incarnation."[35]

Patmore's theories of dipodes and catalexis reflect deeper rhythms than his essay purports to deal with. A passage from a 1965 lecture of Frank Kermode sets out the beginning of a theory of fiction which seems strangely akin to what Patmore obscurely intuited as a response to an interiorly perceived rhythm of experience. Patmore notices "There is no charm in the rhythm of monotones. . . . The ticking of a clock is truly monotonous; but when we listen to it, we hear, or rather seem to hear, two, or even four, distinct tones, upon the imaginary distinction of which, and the equally imaginary emphasis of one or two, depends what we call its rhythm."[36] Frank Kermode draws on the same image:

Let me take . . . the ticking of a clock. We ask what it says and we can agree that it says *tick-tock*. . . . *Tick* is our word for a physical beginning, *tock* our word for an end. . . . What enables them to be different is a special kind of middle. We can perceive a duration only when it is organized. It can be shown by experiment that subjects who listen to rhythmic structures such as *tick-tock*, repeated identically, can reproduce the interval within the structure accurately, but they cannot grasp spontaneously the interval between the rhythmic groups, that is, between *tock* and *tick*, even when this remains constant. The first interval is organized and limited, the second not.[37]

Kermode, talking about plot in fiction, distinguishes between "an organization that humanizes time by giving it form" (tick to tock) and "purely successive time of the sort that we need to humanize" (tock to tick). Patmore senses the need to order experience more comprehensively by discerning (naming, controlling) the "time" from tick to tick.

II   *The Later Prose*

Although Patmore had more or less officially closed his poetic career with the 1879 collective edition of his poems (1886 was the "final" edition, however), his literary life was not over. After five years of relative silence—years of profound personal loss in the deaths of his second wife, his daughter Emily, and his son Henry, but also of new joy in his third marriage and the birth of another son— Patmore rediscovered the public press as a forum in which to air his opinions. Frequent short articles from his pen covered a variety of topics between 1885 and 1888, tapering off in the early 1890s until his death in 1896.

The period of early prose had practically concluded by 1860 with his last *North British Review* article on "Recent Poetry." There were two pieces in *Macmillan's Magazine*, "William Barnes, the Dorsetshire Poet" (1862) praising a too little known writer whom Patmore admired and visited and wrote about at least twice more in the 1880s, and "Mrs. Cameron's Photographs" (1866) featuring the very original work of the sister of Mrs. Jackson who took in the little Patmore girls during their mother's last illness. An 1872 article on a recurring architectural topic, "The Gothic Revival," marked Patmore's first appearance in the *Pall Mall Gazette*, which soon (1875–1877) published several of his odes. A brief review in the *Spectator* (20 March 1875) of Swinburne's edition of the works of George Chapman (the Elizabethan poet and translator of Homer whom Keats celebrated in a famous sonnet) is as far as we know Patmore's last periodical piece for a decade.

His only other publications during this time were the 1877 biography of Bryan Waller Procter (Barry Cornwall), subtitled "an Autobiographical Fragment and Biographical Notes" and actually not much more than that, and a translation of *St. Bernard on the Love of God* which was two thirds the work of Mary Patmore, completed and seen through the press by Coventry in 1881 after her death. The Procter book was a response in friendship to the request of the subject's widow. The Procters had known Patmore's father and had been kind to Coventry from his impecunious twenties to the country gentleman days of his second marriage. The St. Bernard must have been a congenial duty of piety because the mystical writings of the saint had much to say to the poet of the Psyche odes.

The impetus for the new spate of periodical prose (1885–1895)— over a hundred short pieces for the *St. James's Gazette* and a score of articles and reviews in *Fortnightly*, *Anti-Jacobin* and *Merry England*—was political exasperation prompting Patmore to reopen correspondence with Frederick Greenwood, editor of the *St. James's Gazette* at that time and a fellow opponent of Gladstone. This Tory evening paper was by no means exclusively political, and the Patmore articles it carried covered more literary and artistic than strictly political topics.

Patmore considered his *St. James's* essays the fruit of his mature reflection. He himself decided which of them should be reprinted (with a few from other journals) in book form as *Principle in Art*[38] (1889) and *Religio Poetae* (1893). Frederick Page gathered up a great many more of these essays in *Courage in Politics* (1921). The title essay of the first of these collections (*PA*, 1–5) insists that criticism is an act of judgment rather than an expression of feeling. Coleridge, Lessing, Goethe, and Hegel offered principles; many of Patmore's contemporaries contribute only "desultory chatter." Patmore's concrete example of "principle in art" is Augustus Welby Pugin's insistence "that architectural decoration could never be an addition to constructive features, but only a fashioning of them." One may question the practical effectiveness of this dictum as Victorian Gothic got out of hand, but the criterion remains valid.

"Cheerfulness in Life and Art" (*PA*, 6–11) calls for a recognition of the goodness of life without which art is false. By "The Point of Rest in Art" (*PA*, 12–17) Patmore does not mean that point in a picture from which the eye brings the whole into focal proportion, but the *"punctum indifferens* to which all that is interesting is more or less unconsciously referred"—like the unobtrusive character in a drama, say Horatio in *Hamlet*, whose reasonableness makes clear the opposite excesses of the others. "Bad Morality is Bad Art" (*PA*, 18–23) insofar as immorality is inhuman, while law is the "rectitude of humanity" and art is "the constitution of life" whose "grace and sweetness . . . arise from inflection of law" as music demonstrates. "Emotional Art" (*PA*, 24–30, originally "Impressionist Art" in an 1891 *Anti-Jacobin*) at first expostulates against overvaluing the emotional component of poetry—"persuasive music assisting commanding truth to convince" (feminine sensitivity complementing masculine rationality in a typical Patmore analogy) is not didactic but uplifting, from pleasure and pain, through joy and pathos, to ultimate peace. "Peace in Life and Art" (*PA*, 31–36, originally published in *Merry England* in 1892) reiterates the need, for true life and true art, of order (sense subordinate to spirit), joy, and peace. In all of these moral-aesthetic considerations the "present day" suffers from comparison with some earlier period.

"Pathos" (*PA*, 37–43) differs from Aristotelian pity in being simply emotional, whereas pity involves intellect and will. Patmore's examples are of situations—delicately drawn by Hardy, overdone by Dickens—but his point is clearest in this observation: "It is the fact of sunset, not its colours—which are the same as those of sunrise—that constitutes its sadness; and in mere darkness there may be fear and distress, but not pathos." For "Poetical Integrity" (*PA*, 44–49) the touchstone is human significance—"the true light of nature is the human eye." "The Poetry of Negation" (*PA*, 50–54) takes to task the modern poet who yields to turmoil and despondency instead of assuming his proper role of affirmation "of things which it greatly concerns men to know" and which he has power to reveal.

"Distinction" (*PA*, 55–74), a longer essay originally in *Fortnightly Review* in 1890, had caused some furor by its snobbishness ("Democracy hates distinction" and is deficient in culture) and by its damning with faint praise several contemporary writers, of whom "Mrs. Meynell, alone, is . . . almost always thoroughly distinguished." How the article embarrassed her we have already seen (p. 100 above). "Keats" (*PA*, 75–81), a review of Sidney Colvin's book, has similar lapses—"from the comparatively worthless waste of the rest of Keats's writing, Mr. Colvin picks out with accurate discernment the few pieces and passages of real excellence." Patmore goes on to apply his familiar classifications: masculine-truth-power-passion complemented by feminine-beauty-sweetness. Keats is found wanting in masculine (superior) qualities. Patmore assures us that "the femininity of such poets as [Keats and Shelley] is a glorious and immortal gift," but states as fact that only masculine poets can write "classics." "What Shelley Was" (*PA*, 82–91) is less a review of Edward Dowden's biography of the poet than complaints about the misconduct of "a beautiful, effeminate, arrogant boy" whose poetry is "all splendour and sentiment and sensitiveness, and little or no true wisdom or true love." This essay and "Blake" (*PA*, 92–97), which is even more contemptuous, one wishes had not been reprinted.

"Rossetti as a Poet" (*PA*, 98–105), on the other hand, receives careful criticism reviewing good points—thought, clarity of perception, "high aims deeply and characteristically felt"—and bad—"tense without being intense," technically flawed. A most Patmorean comment about Rossetti's constant theme of love notes that it is "not the English love whose stream is steady affection and only its occasional eddies passion." Another limitation in Patmore's eyes is that Rossetti is essentially Italian, and his inherited language compared to English is as a flute to an organ! "Arthur Hugh Clough" (*PA*, 106–12) too rarely "got out of his slough of introspection and doubt," but his "Bothie of

Tober-na-Vuolich" is an enduring poem, heathy, human, and original.

In "Emerson" (*PA*, 113–21), about whom Patmore had written more appreciatively forty years before, we are more than ever conscious of Patmore as phrase-maker—not that he was, here or elsewhere, trying to be clever at his subject's expense, but as senior seer with a penchant for spice, writing for a friendly editor and an urbane readership, Patmore sometimes showed more rhetoric than critical tact. Personal bias is a strong factor in his pronouncements. That Emerson "had neither passion nor appetite" is not just opinion but very nearly accusation. Though a good man, Emerson "had little or no conscience. He admired good, but did not love it; he denounced evil, but did not hate it"—"Emerson's was a sweet and uniformly sunny spirit; but the sunshine was that of the long polar day, which enlightens but does not fructify." Yet for Patmore, Emerson's life and less formal writings (letters and journals) redeem some of the ethereal inconsistencies of the essays and lectures, and Patmore's final strictures regarding Emerson's ability to satisfy an English audience mollify the note of condescension.

Before Patmore leaves the poets of his century (and of the end of the preceding) he ticks off Coleridge (great) and Burns (small) as likely to endure; Byron and Wordsworth as of fluctuating fame; Moore, Rogers, Southey, Cowper, Campbell, Scott as vanishing figures; Crabbe as much more significant than anyone (but Patmore) thinks, especially in comparison with Shelley in terms of reality ("Crabbe and Shelley"—*PA*, 122–28). Another relatively neglected poet, William Barnes, is written up at length as "A Modern Classic" (*PA*, 129–45, originally in *Fortnightly Review* in 1886), that is, one who writes only "under the sense of a subject that makes its own form, and of feelings which form their own words." This particular article is marred by gratuitous lapses of task or judgment: "a man may, like Herrick or Blake, be little better than a blank in intellect"; in America religion "though widespread, is of a vulgarer and less efficient type than among us; art is absolutely non-existent." Barnes is more directly assessed—as "a little rill of bright and perennial beauty"—in two *St. James's* pieces which Patmore did not choose to reprint but which Frederick Page perceptively retrieved for *Courage in Politics* (118–126).[39] Two days after Barnes's death in October 1886, Patmore paid tribute to the rural clergyman who wrote lyric, idyll, and eclogue with the consummate art of Horace; these poems in Dorset dialect were recited to and appreciated by those he also preached to in it. A year or so later Patmore reviewed Barnes's daughter's insufficiently animated and "grievously 'padded'" biography of the Dorset man who himself "wrote nothing but his best." This mark of integrity Patmore had claimed for himself in the preface of his 1886 collected poems: "I have written little, but it is all my best." Said of his poetry, this is true. In Patmore's prose, however, especially the later essays, there are lapses of taste and self-criticism wanes.

The essay on "Mrs. Meynell" (*PA*, 146–58, originally in *Fortnightly Review* in 1892) is a curious mixture of Patmore's theory of the sexes and extravagant praise for "one of the very rarest products of nature and grace—a woman of genius." We may be glad to note that although her true, beautiful, and almost faultless verse, as a woman's, cannot "attain the classical standard," her essays do. Patmore chooses excerpts to illustrate her perfect style and wherever possible any of his prejudices she happens to share, for instance, toward "decivilised" Americans and others. A review of Alice Meynell's *New Essays*, in *Saturday Review* in June 1896, the last year of Patmore's life and after she had tried to quell his ardor, is still ecstatic in her praise— Frederick Page included this article in *Courage in Politics*. It contains a Patmorean "rule" about the "difference between prose, of which the unit is the iambic *foot*, and verse, of which the lowest division is the *metre*, of two feet." One of Mrs. Meynell's excellences is her freedom from the artistic error of slipping from the "unequalled grace of her *walk* into a passage of *dance*." Patmore introduces into the midst of the discussion of prose a bit of private business: he quotes as an example of "unapproachable beauty" comparable to Keats's "Belle Dame sans Merci" a lyric lately printed anonymously, identifying it as Mrs. Meynell's. It is "Why wilt thou chide, / Who hast attained to be denied?" His public admiration is his covert acknowledgment that the message of noble consolation is for himself. The long essay on "Madame de Hautfort" (*PA*, 159–91, originally in *Merry England* in 1893) is a kindred piece although its seventeenth-century subject, a virtuous and beautiful maid of honor at the court of Louis XIII, is not a literary lady. Patmore opens with a discourse on fine manners as a fine art (not accessible, incidentally, to "the poor and socially obscure"), and closes with a plea for a proper complementarity of the sexes which for him means that women should be both subordinate and worshiped.

"A Spanish Novelette" (*PA*, 192–98, originally in *Fortnightly* in 1892), Juan Valers's *Pepita Jimenez*, came to Patmore's notice as one of the "translations of remarkable foreign novels" which his friend Edmund Gosse was editing. Patmore's praise is for its plain spoken naturalness and freedom from "the cant of Manichean purity" which made Victorians prudish. Patmore "On Obscure Books" (*PA*, 199–204) reminds us, as a good librarian should, that reading is a way "of keeping company with the best minds" even if in translation (indirectly excusing his own deficiency in Greek and Latin). In "Shall Smith Have a Statue?" Patmore warns against "premature insistence upon the verdict of fame."

Principle in Art concludes with a cluster of architectural essays from the *St. James's Gazette* in the last quarter of 1886. Patmore hails the "quiet rejoicing in strength, solidity, and permanence" with which carved cornices even in a "cottage built mightily" can suggest the thickness of its walls. Old English delight in chimneys, and the variety resulting from additions to a house over generations are features of architectural character which it is folly or fraud to duplicate in a modern building. A five-part lesson on Egyptian, Greek, pointed Gothic, Norman, and Moresque architectural styles reviews what Patmore had written thirty-five years before but still stood by. A few other *St. James's* pieces in the same vein, which Patmore did not include in *Principle in Art*, Frederick Page uses to round off *Courage in Politics:* "Expression in Architecture," "Architecture and Architectural Criticism," "Liverpool Cathedral," "Churches and Preaching-Halls." These deal with the appropriateness of Gothic and refer frequently to Ruskin, whether in agreement or not. In one essay, "Japanese Houses," Patmore is definitely out of his own territory; one wishes Page had not reprinted his remarks about the Japanese "luxury of unsuperfluousness" as "the result of an extremely limited civilization which knows few wants" (*CP*, 198).

The title essay of Page's collection and a half dozen others dealing with or alluding largely to public affairs are hardly popular. Patmore suggests that "the tonic touch of a great misfortune" is needed to reinvigorate the national mind; the Conservative party (Patmore's own) has failed successively in courage, insight, and intellectual ability; sympathy for those whom we cannot really help can become "a nauseous and vicious effeminacy"; one should not call a fool a fool except in the hope of converting him, if "his conversion is of consequence"; the pope, without temporal power, could be the umpire in international disputes, giving reasons for settlements "similar in form and exhaustiveness" to those accompanying the promulgation of a dogma. Collections of proverbs, instead of being "epitomes of popular wisdom . . . are the stupidest and dullest of all stupid and dull reading."

Literature and landscape are Patmore's most convincing and instructive topics. "December in Garden and Field" and "Old Coach Roads" are genially perceptive. Aesthetic enrichment is "A Safe Charity" and a human gift for the deprived. Many of the short articles Page chooses were, if not actually reviews, occasioned by recently published books. A new edition of *Religio Medici* prompts an appreciation of Sir Thomas Browne, whose name Patmore often evokes as an example of good English prose. Austin Dobson's *Life of Goldsmith*, Hall Caine's *Life of Coleridge*, and the *Memorials of Coleorton* (letters of Coleridge, the Wordsworths, and others) provide subjects for discussion. Contemporary writers—Hardy, Robert Bridges, Aubrey De Vere, Thomas Woolner (poet as well as sculptor), Francis Thompson, Mrs. Walford (a little known novelist)—Patmore praises where he can, and not extravagantly, as one professional speaking to or of another.

A change of subject, "Dreams," has a modern ring: "Dreams have not yet had their due in the systems either of moralists or psychologists" (*CP*, 97). Swedenborg, who had gripped Patmore's imagination thirty years before, is presented again in 1886 as "perhaps the most inscrutable figure in the whole sphere of literature." Honored as a scientist by the King of Sweden, Swedenborg anticipated astronomical discoveries of other galaxies, and in physiology postulated the circulation of the blood before Harvey. His religious writings contain "diamonds of thought in settings of lead" (*CP*, 101). A review of Hegel's and Michelet's *Philosophy of Art* is a plea for "true criticism" which cannot teach an artist "what to do or how to do it; but it can teach him what to avoid" (*CP*, 107).

Although Frederick Page may seem to have been overzealous in reprinting so many more of Patmore's slighter articles than the writer himself saw fit to preserve, this picture of the aging man of letters abreast of current publishing and ready with tart comment from his storehouse of opinions is another reminder of the life-loving productivity of the Hastings period. The sixty-year-old father of an infant son had indeed things to say and vigor enough to say them.

Patmore's weightiest last words are surely the essays collected in *Religio Poetae*[40] (1893 was the only edition in his lifetime). Although fourteen of the twenty-one are reprinted from the same periodicals that *Principle in Art* was drawn from, we have here to some extent a different order of thought—ideas, not personalities; reflections, not reviews; interpretation, not recording or summarizing. Here is whatever can be called "originality" after nearly seventy years of reading and observation and absorption and reaction by a keen intellect and a highly developed sensibility that made imperious claims upon experience and stamped it "Patmore."

The title essay (*RP*, 1–9) implicitly recalls the *Religio Medici* of Sir Thomas Browne whose integrity and style Patmore often held up as exemplary. Patmore comes quickly to his point that the poet is primarily a *perceiver* (not an Emersonian *seer*) whose *real apprehension* or taking hold of reality (which may be too big to embrace or "comprehend") enables him to treat "spiritual realities as the concrete and very credible things they truly are," translating them into their likenesses in external nature which can be really apprehended by the nonpoet. No vague "fire-mist" or "unintelligent heat" can replace authentic perception.

"The Precursor" (*RP*, 10–17) restates Patmore's basic theme that the love between God and the soul can best be understood through its analogue, the love between bridegroom and bride. St. John the Baptist, the precursor of Christ, is brought in as representing the relation of natural to divine love. Patmore enlarges upon the allegorical significance of the Baptist's food and accoutrements, pointing to a more extensive application of scriptural passages to Patmore's favorite analogy of natural and divine love. Enigma and myth are commonly "The Language of Religion" (*RP*, 18–30) after the early stages of the soul's progress. The very roots of language show a blend of phonetic and objective imagery. It is natural to use symbols and parables and ritual to cloak from the unprepared and reveal to the enlightened the exacting truths of divine communication. "Attention" (*RP*, 31–37), or "the capacity for looking steadily at realities worthy of being reasoned about," is lamentably rare; without it there is no communion with Wisdom. In reminding his contemporaries of these almost forgotten truths, Patmore speaks equally to later generations who are rediscovering allegory and symbol and meditation.

"Christianity an Experimental Science" (*RP*, 38–45) refers explicitly to religious experience vouchsafed to one who is "*perfectly sincere and faithful.*" In "A People of Stammering Tongue" (*RP*, 46–50) Patmore avers that an aphoristic manner is the most proper in speaking of the things of the spirit, for the highest knowledge is "nuptial," a "knowledge of fruition, for which there is no intelligible word nor 'reason.'" "The Bow Set in the Clouds" (*RP*, 51–56) is probably more readable today than in the 1890s. Patmore begins by defending his position that "some knowledge of Christian mysteries has been enjoyed by individuals in all times and places," especially some inkling of the Incarnation. He goes on to the doctrine of the

Trinity, bringing in Plato's three sexes, the parable of Teiresias, and his own version of man in Genesis "containing" the woman.

The snobbish note returns in "Christianity and 'Progress'" (*RP*, 57–63, originally in *Fortnightly Review* in 1892). Cautioning against material happiness as a criterion for the success or failure of Christianity, Patmore takes an elitist position—it is true not only that "few are chosen," but that few qualify. Of the three kinds of "Simplicity" (*RP*, 64–67), of the child, of genius, and of wisdom, only the last is free of concomitant defects. There is a certain consistency in Patmore's counterromantic statements. He rarely condemns outright in literary contexts, but is explicit in his preference for rationality, control, and other classical qualities, often in terms of the masculine-feminine polarity he is fond of citing.

"Ancient and Modern Ideas of Purity" (*RP*, 68–71) deplores puritanism as unhealthy—"it was impurity which first brought fig-leaves into fashion." "Conscience" (*RP*, 72–76) deals again with "the twofold constitution of man," the female component being "not a vice, but a virtue without sufficient light." "Real Apprehension" (*RP*, 77–84) invoked in the essay "Religio Poetae" is "emphatically the quality which constitutes 'good sense.'" Newman is named among others as possessing the quality, but nowhere does Patmore stress its affinity to Newman's "real" as distinct from "notional" assent. "Seers, Thinkers and Talkers" (*RP*, 85–95) hails intellect which "discerns truth as a living thing" and calls "wisdom in the conduct of life" the highest genius. Patmore is in effect pleading for philosopher kings who however "are the last to come to the front in states of ultra-popular government." "Possibilities and Performances" (*RP*, 96–101) seems, not untypically, to belittle science and plead for the recognition of "prophetic moments."

"Imagination" (*RP*, 102–7) as the "language of genius" seizes on likenesses by which things "'unseen are known by the . . . seen.'" "The Limitations of Genius" (*RP*, 108–12) points out that a certain narrowness is a strength when it keeps an artist to his own line of excellence. "A Pessimist Outlook" (*RP*, 113–20) and "Thoughts on Knowledge, Opinion, and Inequality" (*RP*, 121–38), both from the *Fortnightly Review* although five years apart, review Patmore's anti-democratic prejudices at considerable length.

"Love and Poetry" (*RP*, 139–46) demands that the true poet be something of a mystic, with a sense of the sacramentality of love and nature. "The greatest and perhaps the only real use of natural science is to supply similes and parables for poets and theologians." "The

Weaker Vessel" (*RP*, 147–58), originally two *St. James's* articles, the second of which was entitled "Why Women are Dissatisfied," contains Patmore's most extreme statement of his view of male-female complementarity: "To maintain that man and woman are equals in intelligent action is just as absurd as it should be to maintain that the hand that throws a ball and the wall that casts it back are equal." "Dieu et ma Dame" (*RP*, 159–75) is a fuller development of Patmore's pervasive analogy: God is to soul as husband is to wife.

Coventry Patmore's delight in aphorisms is evident even in his longer prose passages. In his final tidying up of his writings the year before he died, he gathered, lest they be lost, about two hundred pages of short sayings and paragraphs under four heads: "Aurea Dicta," "Knowledge and Science," "Homo," "Magna Moralia." Together these constitute the 1895 volume, *The Rod, the Root, and the Flower*; its title page bears two Scripture quotations whose prophetic ring is messianic, incarnational, suggestive of promise and fulfillment: "There shall come forth a rod out of the root of Jesse, and a flower shall rise up out of his root" (Isaiah 11:1); "My covenant shall be in your flesh" (Genesis 17:13).

The "golden sayings" section is a sort of commonplace book, with some acknowledged quotations (Goethe, John of the Cross, Augustine, Plutarch, Sallust, Aristotle), other entries that appear to be reading notes (as from Swedenborg), many Patmore "originals" and poetic fragments: "So give me to possess this mystery that I shall not desire to understand it" (*R*, 10); "Our thoughts and feelings are modifications of our spiritual substance, and the soul, as a phonograph, retains them all forever, to lie tacit or to be summoned at need" (*R*, 11); "Great contemplatives are infallible, so long as they only affirm. When they begin to prove, any fool can confute them" (*R*, 23); "How fair a flower is sown / When Knowledge goes, with fearful tread, / To the dark bed / Of the divine Unknown!" (*R*, 38).

"Knowledge and Science," three dozen longer paragraphs of more consistently theological bearing, include some self-quotation and some Patmorean climaxes: "all knowledge but the knowledge of God is vanity" (*R*, 64); "all knowledge, worthy of the name, is nuptial knowledge" (*R*, 65).

"Homo" reiterates frequently and with some little variation Patmore's theory of the sexes: "The external man and woman are each the projected *simulacrum* of the latent half of the other, and they do but love themselves in thus loving their opposed likeness" (*R*, 99).

In "Magna Moralia" Patmore martials his arguments and paradoxes with more effort at persuasiveness and fewer scoldings than hitherto. In his mood of reconciliation he sees the "Visible Church" as "the larva of the caddis-fly, from which the winged truth shall finally emerge, perfect and beautiful, but which at present inhabits a house of singular grotesqueness" (*R*, 187). He also notes that the "Catholic Church itself has been nearly killed by the infection of the puritanism of the Reformation" which identifies sex with impurity, failing to understand "the greatest of all graces and means of grace" (*R*, 201). It is fitting and hardly unexpected that the last paragraph of Patmore's last book should exalt nuptial love. At this point he expresses unaccustomed hope that "Catholic psychology" will line itself up on his side.

CHAPTER 8

Conclusion

APPRECIATION of Patmore across the channel became visible only after his death. His French admirers were kindred spirits. Paul Claudel's acquaintance with Patmore's work, limited he tells us[1] to the *Unknown Eros*, dates from a meeting with Algar Thorold[2] in 1900 at Solesmes where both were making a retreat at the Benedictine monastery. Two themes in Patmore appealed strongly to Claudel: the horror of the infinite (Patmore's "Legem Tuam Dilexi" opens: "The 'Infinite.' Word horrible! at feud / With life and the braced mood / Of power and joy and love"), and the spiritual nuptials of the soul with God. During the next decade, which embraced the period of Claudel's *Cinq Grandes Odes* wherein these themes figure, he kept coming back to Patmore and began a series of translations of Patmore odes, some of which appeared in the Belgian periodical *Antée* (1906) and in *Nouvelle Revue Française* (1911). That these are preserved in the Pléiade edition of Claudel's *Oeuvre Poétique*[3] shows that the translator regarded them as more than mere exercises.

Patmore's French vogue was not confined to the odes but included the late prose in the same spirit. Charles Du Bos edited for the quarterly *Vigile* Marthe Nouguier's translations from *Aurea Dicta*, one of the groups of aphorisms which Patmore's last book, *The Rod, the Root, and the Flower* (1895) comprised. Admitting to "un dernier reliquat de jansénisme,"[4] Du Bos eliminated all the sayings that related conjugal love and the union of the Church with God—all that was most important to and distinctive of Patmore, whom he nonetheless cited with easy inevitability as in his lectures at St. Mary's College in 1938. Here he acknowledged that Patmore's "real apprehension" combines "the two great modes of imagination, the concrete . . . and the abstract."[5]

Henri Brémond used as a epigraph to *Prière et Poésie*[6] Patmore's words: "All realities sing; nothing else will."[7] To back up his assertion that poetic experience is a propaedeutic to prayer,

> poetic knowledge attains and unites the poet to realities.
> Not directly to the sovereign reality, God—that is the
> exclusive privilege of mystical knowledge—but to all
> the created real, and . . . indirectly to God himself,

he recommends Wordsworth's *Prelude* "and a few pages of Patmore in *Religio Poetae*,"[8] the identification of the poet's "peculiar position—somewhere between that of a Saint and that of Balaam's Ass."[9] Brémond's knowledge of Patmore is quite independent of Claudel's "discovery" of the English poet. Brémond had spent the first six of his twelve or so years as a Jesuit in England, and retained until their deaths his friendships with George Tyrrell of Modernist memory and with Baron Friedrich von Hügel. He would have read Tyrrell's "Coventry Patmore" in the *Month* for December 1900,[10] and perhaps discussed its original with Tyrrell or von Hügel. The latter was a personal friend of Basil Champneys and had met Patmore through him.

Yet another French writer, Jean Guitton, quoting in his journals[11] lines of Patmore with the easy familiarity of Charles Williams, brings us back to "le poète anglais de l'amour conjugal."[12]

That Patmore wanted to be so known we have no doubt. That he preferred this to be demonstrated ultimately from the later rather than from the earlier work we surmise from his special cherishing of his aphoristic prose (his own "wisdom literature") and of the odes whose sublimity he hoped others would recognize.

Except for the handful of poems written in the 1890s for Alice Meynell,[13] Patmore saw the 1886 *Poems* as "closing [his] task as a poet." His preface to this edition goes on to say: "I have written little, but it is all my best; I have never spoken when I had nothing to say, nor spared time or labour to make my words true. I have respected posterity; and should there be a posterity which cares for letters, I dare to hope that it will respect me."[14]

This modest claim we grant him. Reflecting on his total poetic output we are impressed by the consistency of his love and marriage themes and by his developing craftsmanship. The notes of disdainfulness and political fanaticism that are heard in the later work, and that he considered expressions of righteous wrath, we are inclined to regard with something of the same indulgence or disappointment that we accord to the fulminations against usury in the cantos of Ezra Pound. Patmore and Pound seem to have little enough in common, but each is distinguished by a significant gift of poetry and a need to sit as prophet-judge against a world he has in part withdrawn from. The angry Patmore's conservatism and social prejudice are so extreme as to suggest a caricature of the indignant Victorian gentleman. Caricature has its place, but it is not the vehicle which communicates the essential Patmore. His chosen theme is married love, as in itself a source of joy and strength, and as an analogue to the highest spiritual experience. The theme rings through the human and humorous early narrative poems to the intense and exotic or poignant later odes. Even here the hothouse atmosphere is often lightened by a breath of ordinary air, as in Psyche's "Enough, enough" to Eros, "Undo thine arms and let me see the sky" (*Po*, 431, 432).

Patmore makes paradox work for him; it is rarely a mere ornament, and often a compact expression of his theme. Psyche's plea quoted above is actually a fair summing up of Patmore's vision:

> Have pity of my clay-conceived birth
> And maiden's simple mood,
> Which longs for ether and infinitude,
> As thou, being God, crav'st littleness and earth!

(Po, 431)

Patmore is well within the tradition of Christian mystical writers in speaking of the soul as feminine to God. His aphorisms in *The Rod, the Root, and the Flower* reiterate this in varying degrees of explicitness. The modern reader may weary with the insistence, or share the distaste of Aubrey De Vere, Basil Champneys, and others of Patmore's contemporaries, but it is important to understand the operative metaphor as an attempt to cope artistically with Patmore's central experience of nuptial love and union, and with his authentic Christian desire to deepen his spiritual life which is union with God.

Notes and References

Chapter One

1. Derek Patmore, *Portrait of My Family* (New York, 1935), p. 8.
2. Oliver Miller, *Pictures in the Royal Collection: Tudor, Stuart and Early Georgian* (London, 1963), p. 152.
3. Basil Champneys, *Memoirs and Correspondence of Coventry Patmore* (London, 1900), 1:1.
4. Champneys, 1:6.
5. The fullest account of P. G. Patmore available still seems to be that of Valéry Larbaud, *Ce Vice Impuni* (Paris, 1925), pp. 117ff.
6. Hazlitt's biographers tend to blacken P. G. Patmore. Catherine Macdonald Maclean claims that he "shabbied everything he touched on, in literature as in life" (*Born under Saturn: A Biography of William Hazlitt* [New York, 1944], p. 531) and Augustine Birrell's English Men of Letters *William Hazlitt* (New York, 1902) speaks of "the undesirable Patmore" as playing "a dubious part in Hazlitt's life" (pp. 178, 223). The distaste arises from Patmore's seeming encouragement of Hazlitt's liaison with the maid in his lodging house, the subject of the letters which constituted Hazlitt's tasteless *Liber Amoris* (1823). In 1822 Hazlitt and Patmore made the rounds of important picture collections together and published their observations independently: Hazlitt in the *London Magazine* throughout 1823 and later in book form; Patmore in Colburn's *New Monthly Magazine* and in a book, *British Galleries of Art*, in 1824 ahead of Hazlitt's.
7. See Victor, Count de Soligny (pseud.), *Letters on England* (London, 1823); *Imitations of Celebrated Authors* (London, 1826); in later life the notorious *My Friends and Acquaintance*, 3 vols. (London, 1854), reviewed unfavorably in three columns of the *Times*, 19 August 1854.
8. *Chatsworth; or, the Romance of a Week* (London, 1844) is a "new Decameron" of retold tales from Chaucer, Heywood, Shakespeare, Spanish drama, with a preliminary description of the several guests who tell the stories at the house party at Chatsworth—D'Israeli, Bulwer Lytton, Mrs. Gore, the Honorable Mrs. Norton, and Coventry as the "Boy Poet" are recognizable under their disguises.
9. Champneys, 2:41–56. This is not a completely accurate transcription. The original among the Patmore papers in Boston College Library has, for instance (speaking of Swedenborg's psychology), "drawn from the great Catholic doctors with whom he seems to have been well acquainted."

Champneys (unless of course he was using another autograph copy with a variant reading) edits this (p. 52) to read ". . . doctrines with which. . . ."

10. *Portrait of My Family*. p. 42.

11. In the private collection of A.F.P. Watts, grandson of Coventry's youngest daughter, Gertrude.

12. Champneys, 1:36.

13. See Matthew Whiting Rosa, *The Silver-Fork School*, Columbia University Studies in English and Comparative Literature, no. 123 (New York, 1936), pp. 117ff. Mrs. Gore was prominent enough to be parodied by Thackeray in "Punch's Prize Novelists" in a serial called "Lords and Liveries. By the authoress of 'Dukes and Dejeuners,' 'Hearts and Diamonds,' 'Marchionesses and Milliners,' etc." (*Punch* 12 [1847]: 237–38, 247, 257–58).

14. Champneys, 1:36.

15. Ibid., 1:41.

16. John Cowie Reid, *Mind and Art of Coventry Patmore* (London, 1957), p. 19.

17. Champneys, 1:39.

18. Ibid., 2:48.

19. Ibid., 1:45, 49.

20. Ibid., 1:viii.

21. To Mother St. Ignatius Wheaton, 8 April 1915, in "Coventry Patmore in the Correspondence of his Contemporaries," ed. Sister Mary Anthony Weinig (M.A. thesis, Fordham University, 1951), p. 66.

22. Champneys, 1:vii.

23. Edmund Gosse, *Coventry Patmore* (New York, 1905), p. vi.

24. (London, 1949), p. 121.

25. Mrs. Vigers, sister of Samuel Laman Blanchard (1803/4–1845), took Emily Andrews to Germany at least once, in 1845, the year of Blanchard's tragic suicide. This "honestest and kindest of men who ever lived by pen," whose wit "had the wonderful knack of never hurting anybody," and "who practiced the most singular art of discovering good qualities in people" (Thackeray's tribute, "A Brother of the Press on the History of a Literary Man," reprinted from *Fraser's Magazine*, March 6, 1846, in the *Critical Papers in Literature* volume of the Harry Furniss Centenary Edition of Thackeray's *Works* [London, 1911], pp. 332–49—bibliographical note by Lewis Melville, p. xiii), was a good friend of Douglas Jerrold and knew P. G. Patmore.

26. Georgiana Andrews, called "Georgina" and described as a "stunner" in Holman Hunt's and Millais's letters, visited Oxford in 1853 where Hunt fell briefly in love with her. But during the next year Millais wrote to Hunt in the Middle East: "One thing I fear to relate because I know your tender heart was once moved by her charms. Miss Georgina Andrews is no longer single. This morning I received wedding cards from Mr. and Mrs. Thomas Patmore— South American sugar planter brother [of Coventry Patmore]" (Diana Holman-Hunt, *My Grandfather: His Wives and Loves*, [New York, 1969],

pp. 88, 95, 127). Aside from the wrong Christian names and continent this corresponds to what we already know of Coventry's young sister-in-law, and fills in more background with a Pre-Raphaelite flavor.

27. Champneys, 1:128. Mrs. Orme had been Elizabeth Barrett Browning's governess for a while at Hope End in the Malvern Hills (some time after 1810) and remained a sort of literary preceptress to her, at least to the extent of showing Elizabeth's poems to Richard Hengist Horne for his opinion in the late 1830s (Gardner B. Taplin, *Life of Elizabeth Barrett Browning* [New Haven, 1957] pp. 8, 83). See also W. Robertson Nicoll and Thomas J. Wise, eds., *Literary Anecdotes of the Nineteenth Century* (London, 1896), pp. 377–84.

28. Frederick Page, who offers an interesting and tenable theory that the earlier *Odes* were originally to be part of the sequel to the published four parts of the *Angel in the House*, as some of the poems in the 1853 *Tamerton Church-Tower* were part of the yet to appear book 1 of the *Angel*, cautions us against reading *The Toys* too literally as referring to Milnes who was fourteen when his mother died. It could well have been prompted by an incident in Milnes's childhood—Coventry himself says so (Champneys, 2:271)—but shaped as a poem for the continuation of Frederick's story after Jane's death in the *Victories of Love*, the fourth part of the *Angel* (*Patmore: a Study in Poetry* [London, 1933], pp. 109–10).

29. Champneys, 1:158.

30. British Library Add. Ms. 46145, ff. 4–9.

31. Bodleian Ms. Don. e. 72.

32. Letter in Boston College Library, Patmore Collection. E. J. Oliver (*Coventry Patmore* [New York, 1956], pp. 68–70) reads Conrad's *Chance* (1913) as picking up and enlarging the relationship of the sailor son (the hero, Captain Anthony) and the poet father ("a savage sentimentalist"). Valéry Larbaud (*Ce Vice Impuni*, pp. 52, 274) adverts in a short review of *Chance* to the unmistakable description of a famous writer. An unpublished letter of Frederick Page to Derek Patmore (Princeton University Library, Patmore Collection) speaks of the biographical chapters written but not included in Page's *Patmore: A Study in Poetry*. One on "The Father in the House," Page says, "shatters the caricature of C P as 'Anthony Caerleon' [*sic*] in Conrad's *Chance*."

33. Unpublished letter owned by Gurney Patmore's descendants.

34. See especially the end of Francis Patmore's recollections, *English Review* 54 (1932): 135–41.

35. *Principle in Art* (London, 1898), p. 98.

36. Letter in Boston College Library, Patmore Collection.

37. Champneys, 1:150–53.

38. Ibid., 1:102.

39. Ibid., 1:103.

40. Ibid., 1:146.

41. Ibid., 1:282.

42. See Reid, *Mind and Art of Coventry Patmore* and Alfred Thomas, "The Literary Criticism of Coventry Patmore" (M.A. thesis, University of London, 1960), for identifiable Patmore criticism of Tennyson.

43. Letters of Thomas Woolner to Coventry Patmore (1860–1890), Princeton University Library.

44. Champneys, 2:308–309.

45. See below, chapter 2.

46. See Champneys, 2:318–28.

47. Ibid., 1:82–83.

48. *Letters of George Meredith to Alice Meynell, 1896–1907* (London, 1923), p. 9.

49. Wheaton, "Psyche and the Prophet," *Catholic World* 118 (1925): 355–66.

50. See eight articles in *St. James's Gazette* for May and June 1885. These came out in book form, *How I Managed and Improved my Estate*, in 1886.

51. Champneys, 1:324.

52. *Further Letters of Gerard Manley Hopkins including his Correspondence with Coventry Patmore*, ed. Claude Colleer Abbott (London, 1838), p. 207.

53. Champneys, 1:361.

54. Osbert Burdett, *The Idea of Coventry Patmore* (London, 1921), p. 178.

55. "Distinction," in *Principle in Art*, p. 67.

56. British Library Add. Ms. 46145.

57. J. W. Robertson Scott, *The Story of the Pall Mall Gazette* (London, 1950), pp. 386–96.

58. Champneys, 2:296–97.

59. *Our Pets and Playfellows* (London, 1880), p. 40.

60. Champneys, 1:296.

61. *Coventry Patmore*, pp. 140ff.

62. Louise Wheaton et al., *A Daughter of Coventry Patmore: Sister Mary Christina, SHCJ* (London, 1924).

63. The recurring "Joshua" may be explained in terms of her father's scriptural exegesis as ultimately formalized in *The Rod, the Root, and the Flower* (London: Bell, 1895), "Homo," XXX, p. 135: "Joshua represents the power of God in the conquest and conversion of the natural man." (The book is hereafter cited as *R*.) A simpler Joshua reference, which Emily would have known in its published form, is in the last prelude to the first canto of the *Angel in the House* where Joshua retrieves the promised land (rich and heathen) for the people of God, as the Christian poet takes over the field of love from courtly bards who sing of adultery.

64. *Daughter of Coventry Patmore*, pp. 76–90.

65. "By Emily's little book of Verses do you mean the one she did on purpose for me, and has the verses to Honoria included in it? If so it is mine alone, therefore I have every right to do as I like with it. Therefore I say, *Yes* dear Mother St. Ignatius, do take them . . ." (letter of December 1919 to

Emily's biographer, quoted in Weinig, p. 76). Also, "Do you think I am asking too much dear, if I ask you to omit the letter that I sent you about our marriage? I know I sent it to you, but I would rather that Honoria was an unknown quantity" (Weinig, p. 70). The letter in question is quoted in *Daughter*, pp. 145–46, but with omissions. The original is in the Princeton Patmore Collection along with correspondence about Derek Patmore's work on his great grandfather.

66. Weinig, p. 67.

67. Paul Chapman, M.D., "A Reminiscence of Coventry Patmore," *Nineteenth Century* 56 (1904): 672.

68. A somewhat aggrieved article by George Trobridge, "Coventry Patmore and Swedenborg," *Westminster Review* 165 (1906): 76–90, parallels passages in Patmore's writings with excerpts from "the Seer" in a conscientious reading of the former's as a paraphrase of Swedenborg's *Marriage Love* and other works of like import. The alleged failure of Patmore's advocates to acknowledge this indebtedness appears to be the sore point. There are, however, numerous references to Swedenborg as one of the many Patmorean enthusiasms in all the fuller accounts of the poet's thought. See also Patmore's own articles on Swedenborg: *Fraser's Magazine* 55 (1857): 174–82; *National Review* 6 (1858): 336–59; an 1886 *St. James's Gazette* piece reprinted in Frederick Page's collection of Patmore prose, *Courage in Politics* (London, 1921), pp. 101–5. Patmore's annotated copy of the two-volume *Index* to Swedenborg's *Arcana Coelestia* (London, 1865) is in the Boston College Library's Patmore Collection. Acutally the passages Trobridge feels Patmore has plagiarized are expressive of ideas not particularly original with Swedenborg either, but shared by idealizers of Christian marriage before and after the era of unwholesome prudery against which Patmore inveighed as unnatural, unsound, and fundamentally uncatholic.

69. Champneys, 1:252.

70. Ibid., 1:254.

71. British Library Add. Ms. 46145, f. 46.

72. British Library Add. Ms. 54347, pp. 310–12. The manuscript diaries run from 54340 to 54348, and have been indexed by R. E. Thompson. Roger Lancelyn Green edited the two-volume *Diaries of Lewis Carroll* (London, 1953).

73. *Fortnightly Review*, January 1894, reprinted in *Courage in Politics*, p. 160.

74. *Alice Meynell: A Memoir* (London, 1929).

Chapter Two

1. Frederick G. Kenyon, ed., *Robert Browning and Alfred Domett* (New York, 1906), p. 107.

2. "Poems by Coventry Patmore," *Ainsworth's Magazine* 6 (1844): 93.

3. "Recent Poetry," *Tait's Edinburgh Magazine* 11 (1844): 727.

4. "[Once] no such volume as Mr. Coventry Patmore's could have ventured to crawl out of manuscript into print. . . . The weakest inanity ever perpetrated in rhyme by the vilest poetaster of any former generation, becomes masculine verse when contrasted with the nauseous pulings of Mr. Patmore's muse. . . . This is the life into which the slime of the Keates [*sic*] and Shelleys of former times has fecundated! The result was predicted about a quarter of a century ago in the pages of this Magazine, and many attempts were made to suppress the nuisance at its fountainhead. . . . nothing is so vivacious as corruption, until it has reached its last stage. . . . now at length attained. Mr. C. Patmore's . . . poetry (thank Heaven!) cannot corrupt into anything worse than itself" (*Blackwood's* 56 July–December 1844): 331–42.

5. *Poems* (London, 1844), pp. 19–20; this edition is hereafter cited as *P*.

6. *Coventry Patmore*, p. 57.

7. Champneys, 1:49.

8. W. M. Rossetti, *Prae-Raphaelite Diaries and Letters* (London, 1900), p. 229.

9. Kathleen Tillotson, *Novels of the Eighteen-forties* (Oxford, 1954), pp. 7ff.

10. From a letter of 1847 quoted in the *Life of Cornelia Connelly, 1809–1879, Foundress of the Society of the Holy Child Jesus*, By a Member of the Society (London, 1922), p. 122. French *was* taught as well as Latin in her schools. Incidentally, Emily Honoria Patmore while still a schoolgirl at St. Leonards (where she later taught as a nun) was once "sent to give a French lesson" to some younger children and apparently carried it off with great success (*A Daughter of Coventry Patmore:*, p. 149).

11. *Poems of Tennyson*, ed. Christopher Ricks, Longmans' Annotated English Poets (London, 1969), p. 601.

12. *Poems of Tennyson*, p. 183. It was first published in 1830.

13. *Edinburgh Review* 102 (1855): 509–10.

14. *Poems of Coventry Patmore*, ed. Frederick Page (London, 1949), p. 460; hereafter cited as *Po*.

15. First published in *Fortnightly Review* 42 (1887): 259–66; reprinted in *Religio Poetae*.

16. William Clyde De Vane, *A Browning Handbook* (New York, 1955), pp. 136–37.

17. *Complete Works of Robert Browning* (Athens, Ohio, 1973), 4:28, 42.

18. All references to this treatise will be to the critical edition with commentary prepared by Sister Mary Augustine Roth as a doctoral dissertation (Catholic University of America, 1961). The essay first appeared as "English Metrical Critics" in *North British Review* 27 (1857): 127–61, and was later included as a "Prefatory Study of English Metrical Law" in *Amelia* (London, 1878).

19. Tennyson's rollicking-solemn and mournful–high-spirited examples of Patmore's precepts are quoted by Hallam Tennyson, *Alfred Lord Tennyson: a Memoir* . . . (New York, 1898), p. 470.

20. W. Holman Hunt, *Pre-Raphaelitism and the Pre-Raphaelite Brotherhood* (London, 1905), 1:159.

21. *Pre-Raphaelitism*, 1:145, 196.

22. *Prae-Raphaelite Diaries and Letters* (London, 1900), p. 221.

23. *P-R Diaries and Letters*, pp. 210, 212.

24. In this year Millais received the baronetcy, an event not alluded to by Holman Hunt who observes in his memoirs of 1873–1887 that "Millais, from the shelter of the Royal Academy, had gained what was an advantage to his professional position, the reputation of having abjured our principles" (*Pre-Raphaelitism*, 2:333).

25. Bodleian Ms. Don. e. 72 f. 37 (Hastings, 30 November 1885).

26. "Millais painted the portrait of Emily Augusta Patmore in 1851 . . . and exhibited it at the Royal Academy in 1852" (2:326); Champneys quotes a letter from Millais to Coventry Patmore, 22 October 1851: "I was delighted to hear of your full satisfaction at Mrs. Patmore's portrait. I am very anxious that Tennyson should see it, that he may give me leave to paint his wife's" (2:327). (The portrait is reproduced in Champneys, vol. 1 facing p. 116.)

27. Edmund Gosse, *Coventry Patmore*, pp. 36–37.

28. *Portrait of My Family*, p. 8, where the date is given as 1861, ten years after the actual date.

29. Champneys, 2:152–53.

30. Entry for November 1849 in *P-R Diaries and Letters*, p. 233.

31. E. T. Cook and Alexander Wedderburn, eds., *Works of John Ruskin*, 39 vols. (London, 1903–1912), 12:319–27. Here also appear two 1854 letters on Hunt's *Awakening Conscience* and *Light of the World*, pp. 328–35, and the long pamphlet on Pre-Raphaelitism, pp. 339–98.

32. Van Akin Burd, ed., *The Winnington Letters: John Ruskin's Correspondence with Margaret Alexis Bell and the Children at Winnington Hall* (Cambridge, Mass., 1969), p. 151.

33. E. T. Cook, *Life of John Ruskin* (London, 1912), 1:287, quotes this and recalls Holman Hunt's feeling "it was written expressly for him."

34. Champneys, 1:83.

35. Diana Holman-Hunt, *My Grandfather*, p. 125.

36. Bodleian MS. Eng.lett.d.40, ff. 34–35.

37. *P-R Diaries and Letters*, p. 290; see also p. 281.

38. Cambridge edition (Boston, 1900), p. 209.

39. *Coventry Patmore*, p. 20.

40. Taplin, pp. 64ff.

41. Taplin, pp. 11, 15, 61, 94.

42. *North British Review* 26 (1857): 444, 446, 449.

43. Bk. 1, lines 438–40. See Paul Turner, "Aurora versus the Angel," *RES* 24 (1948): 227–35, and Champneys, 1:171.

44. "Recent Poetry," *Tait's Edinburgh Magazine* 11 (1844): 726; see also p. 30n.3 above.

Chapter Three

1. Only a few of his sixty or more plays are preserved even in the eight-volume edition of *The Writings of Douglas Jerrold* (London, 1851–1858). Jerrold died in 1857.

2. See, e.g., "How Mr. Chokepear Keeps a Merry Christmas" (1 [1841]: 277), exposing phariseeism; "Groans of the People" (2 [1842]: 88), prodding Sir Robert Peel to do more than "touch his hat;" "Blood" (2 [1842]: 190), against glamorizing murder; "The 'Sabre' and the 'Cross'" (3 [1842]: 251), on the French in Algeria.

3. *DNB*, XI, 830, 832. Austin Dobson's article observes: "As Cruikshank refines upon Gillray and Rowlandson, so Leech refines upon Cruikshank, but to a much greater extent."

4. *Novels of the Eighteen-forties*, p. 30, n.

5. Richard M. Kelly, ed., *The Best of Mr. Punch: The Humorous Writings of Douglas Jerrold* (Knoxville, Tennesee, 1970), pp. 5–6.

6. 9 (July–December 1845): 73. A few issues before no. 214, which carries Patmore's atrocity poem, a full page cartoon (p. 47) of "The Railway Juggernaut of 1845" shows a locomotive labeled "Speculation" with a demon hugging the smokestack and a crowd before it, some prostrate or groveling, some offering money bags. It would not take much imagination to see P. G. Patmore in the victim throng.

7. (London, 1853), pp. 191–98.

8. 9 (July–December 1845): 44, 71, 91.

9. Eyewitness account, quoted in *Annual Register* for 1845, p. 254.

10. *Douglas Jerrold's Shilling Magazine* 2 (1845): 128–32.

11. *Tamerton Church-Tower*, pp. 208–12. An even shorter version, called *A London Fête*, is in the 1949 *Poems* (Oxford edition), pp. 56–57.

12. See also James Pope-Hennessy, *Monckton Milnes: the Years of Promise, 1809–1851* (London, 1949), pp. 128–30, for full account of Thackeray's and Milnes's attendance (with 40,000 other witnesses) at the execution, 7 July 1840, of Courvoisier, the murderer of Lord William Russell.

13. *Tamerton Church-Tower*, p. 147.

14. *Douglas Jerrold's Shilling Magazine* 1 (January–June 1845): 90, 184.

15. Hunt's approbation had spurred Moxon to publish the 1844 *Poems* of P. G.'s son, and had followed the little volume with good advice: "Youngest England should have a care, and not hazard too many accidents by 'flood and field'—too many horsebacks in all weathers and running races with time— Hear this, Coventry Patmore! You who want nothing but experience, and the

study of the mechanisms of verse, to become equal to the finest poets existing" ("A Jar of Honey from Mount Hybla," *Ainsworth's Magazine* 6 [1844]: 491). Champneys (2:32–33) quotes an amusing letter from Patmore when old to Edmund Gosse describing his first interview with the pictures-que Leigh Hunt.

16. Emerson visited England in 1847–1848; his letters and journals mention meeting Patmore the poet and sublibrarian (Ralph Rusk, ed., *Letters of Ralph Waldo Emerson* [New York, 1939–1966], 4:55, 62, 66; *Journals and Miscellaneous Notebooks of Ralph Waldo Emerson*, vol. 10, *1847–1848*, ed. Merton M. Sealts [Cambridge, Mass., 1973], pp. 240, 255, 316, 531, 537, etc.); see also Rusk, *Life of Ralph Waldo Emerson* (New York, 1949), p. 345.

17. *Shilling Magazine* 2 (September 1845): 277; 1 (June 1845): 565.

18. *Shilling Magazine* 2 (September 1845): 283.

19. *Shilling Magazine* 4 (1846): 11. Reid lists this as Patmore's; Frederick Page (*Courage in Politics*, p. 204) is doubtful. Alfred Thomas ("Literary Criticism of Coventry Patmore" [M.A. thesis, University of London, 1960]) rejects it as unverifiable along with all but one of the 1845–1846 ascriptions by J. C. Reid—an "Emerson" in *Lowe's Edinburgh Magazine*. In general it seems safe to rely on Frederick Page's judgment where the evidence is only internal. He knew Patmore's work more thoroughly than did any other critic in the first half of the twentieth century, and, though decidedly an enthusiast, was professionally qualified through long connection with publishing at Oxford University Press. The *Wellesley Index* also questions a few of Reid's attributions, e.g., one *North British Review* assignment is based on an editorial, not authorial, reference to the article's subject as "so fully and recently noticed by us" (Reid, p. 334; *Wellesley Index*, 1:678, Item 387). See also Walter Houghton, "The Authorship of Two Reviews of Arnold's Poetry in the 'North British Review,'" *Victorian Periodicals Newsletter* 8 (1975): 17–20.

20. *Lowe's Edinburgh Magazine* 1 (1846): 171.

21. Champneys, 2:160. See n. 16 above.

22. *Lowe's* 1 (1846): 567.

23. This letter is in the Bodleian (MS. Eng. misc. c. 107, fol. 10) and is published, slightly edited, in Champneys (1: 54–56).

24. *Lowe's* 1 (1846): 575. Abraham Hayward had reviewed the same in the *Edinburgh* 79 (1844): 157–188. See James Pope-Hennessy, *Monckton Milnes: the Years of Promise*, pp. 223–24, for the general English reception of "the famous one-eyed woman writer, Gräfin Ida Hahn-Hahn, who had made the cardinal mistake of bringing to England a male companion and protector" in 1846.

25. *Lowe's* 1 (1846): 228–36, 264–72, 429–38. Frederick Page attributes it to Patmore on strong internal evidence which Kathleen Tillotson accepts ("Donne's Poetry in the Nineteenth Century [1800–1872]" in *Elizabethan and Jacobean Studies Presented to F. P. Wilson* [Oxford, 1959], pp. 307–26), commending the independence and discernment of the articles.

26. *Lowe's* 1 (1846): 229, 230, 233, 266, 434.

27. (London, 1956). See pp. 413, 431–39.

28. Reid follows Praz in citing numerous parallel texts, from Marvell as well as from Donne, with most of the Patmore lines from the *Angel*; John Holloway finds many links in "Patmore, Donne, and the 'Wit of Love,'" *The Charted Mirror* (New York, 1962), pp. 53–62.

29. *The Critic*, no. 5 (January–June 1847): 177.

30. *The Critic*, no. 5 (January–June 1847): 358–59.

31. *British Quarterly Review* 10 (1849): 46–75.

32. *Douglas Jerrold's Shilling Magazine* 4 (1846): 11–16.

33. *British Quarterly Review* 10 (1849): 441–62.

34. (February 1850): 309–53: "Ruskin's Seven Lamps of Architecture"; and (August 1851): 461–96: "Character in Architecture." American and British editions of *North British Review* have different pagination.

35. *British Quarterly Review* 13 (May 1851): 476–96: "Ruskin's *Stones of Venice*"; *Edinburgh Review* 94 (1851): 365–403: "Sources of Expression in Architecture."

36. Champneys, 2:141–65.

37. Champneys, 1:109. The most thorough study of Patmore's specifically literary criticism of the years 1848–1860 and 1885–1896 is Alfred Thomas's thesis (see n. 19 above). Thomas has a particularly carefully verified bibliography, with at least one Patmore item missed by both Page and Reid. Part 4 of Reid's *Mind and Art of Coventry Patmore*, "Aspects of Patmore's Prose," deals severally with his writings on literature, architecture, politics, and prosody.

38. Champneys, 1:64, quoting the letter of the British Museum secretary, 18 November 1846.

39. *Edinburgh Review* 109 (1859): 201–26.

40. Champneys, 2:227.

41. See letter of 18 August 1847 from Coventry Patmore to R. M. Milnes (no. 232 in *The Keats Circle: Letters and Papers 1816–1878*, ed. Hyder Edward Rollins [Cambridge, Mass., 1948], 2:229 and n. 2); see also Sidney Colvin, *John Keats* (New York, 1924), pp. 242–43.

42. *Keats Circle*, 1:cxv, n. 9.

43. Ibid., 2:201.

44. Ibid., 2:205.

45. Champneys, 2:144.

46. Ibid., 1:94.

47. *North British Review* 10 (1848): 69–96.

48. *Keats Circle*, 2:201, 232; *Portrait*, p. 66.

49. Champneys, 1:67; 2:302.

50. Ibid., 2:26.

51. Unpublished letter at the Convent of the Holy Child, Mayfield, Sussex.

52. Champneys, 2:227.

53. *Monckton Milnes: the Years of Promise*, p. 231.

54. Rollins, *Letters of John Keats*, 1:4–6.

55. Champneys, 2:271. See also M. Buxton Forman, *Letters of John Keats* (London, 1952), pp. vii–viii.

56. 1887, in the English Men of Letters Series. See George H. Ford, *Keats and the Victorians*, Yale Studies in English, vol. 101 (New Haven, 1944).

57. *Principle in Art*, pp. 75, 76.

58. Marvel Shmiefsky, "'Principle in Art' as Criticism in the Mainstream," *Victorian Newsletter*, no. 26 (Fall 1964): 28–32.

Chapter Four

1. (London, 1853), where "Church-Tower" is hyphenated. *Tamerton Church-Tower* is hereafter cited as *T*. Most of the quotations from "Tamerton Church-Tower" (the title poem) are from the Oxford edition (*Po*). Significant changes from the 1853 text are noted.

2. In the 1853 version it is not the vicar but "my uncle" who is "learn'd and meek" but weak as Asia and whose daughter is the "all too excellent" Ruth. The vicar exhorts for three quatrains: "Good use have griefs"— "Misfortunes show us sins conceal'd" (p. 46).

3. *Coventry Patmore*, p. 45.

4. See Praz, *Hero in Eclipse in Victorian Fiction*, and above, p. 53

5. 1:146.

6. 1:132.

7. Champneys, 2:159.

8. Ibid.

9. Frederick Page's 1949 Oxford University Press edition incorporated Patmore's "text as he finally revised it" (preface, p. v).

10. Most included the *Victories of Love*, correctly enough, under the title, *Angel in the House*.

11. Patmore's dedication in editions of the *Angel* after 1863. (Emily Augusta Patmore died in 1862.) The anonymous first edition, 1854, bears the following: "The writer of this poem inscribes it to his daughter Emily" (who was one year old). Neither the second nor the third edition has any dedication at all.

12. Only the 1854–1856 edition calls the preliminary poems "accompaniments" and the narrative parts "idyls." Even the 1863 *Angel* has many more "preludes" than Patmore left in after final revision (1886). The Oxford edition (1949) is based on Patmore's 1886 text.

13. *The Betrothal* (1854), p. 7.

14. This title applies to the two-book sequel to the two-book *Angel*, or to the last book alone of the *Angel* considered as four books.

15. Roth, p. 42.

16. "Patmore is not often Dantesque externally (and always Dantean internally)," writes the anonymous reviewer, probably Frederick Page, of Charles Williams's *Figure of Beatrice* in *Notes & Queries* 185 (11 September 1943): 179.

17. The 1854 version expanded the Joshua image into another quatrain, beginning "I've girt myself with thought and prayer" like the leader of the Chosen People. The explicit religious significance strengthens our supposition that the figure of Joshua meant something to Patmore who passed it on to his oldest daughter (see above, chapter 1, n. 63, and *R*, 135).

18. See also canto 10, strophe 5, and canto 12, strophe 4 (pp. 122, 136).

19. *Principle in Art*, pp. 24, 27. The essay quoted, originally published as "Impressionist Art" in the *Anti-Jacobin* in 1891, was reprinted as "Emotional Art."

20. "The Poetry of Negation" in *Principle in Art*, p. 53.

21. This is discussed (still most adequately) by Page (*Patmore—A Study in Poetry* [1933]) and Burdett (*The Idea of Coventry Patmore* [1921]), and aspired to by Charles Williams. Williams's interest in Patmore, whom he quotes often and as a matter of course, was actively encouraged by Page when both worked for Oxford University Press. Frederick Page in a 1915 letter to Emily Patmore's biographer writes: "You are quite welcome to keep those Patmore essays you have. . . . I care as little to make a noise on Patmore's behalf as he did on his own; it is enough to impregnate Williams, and to reinforce your pleasure in him, and anybody else's whom a similar chance brings in my way" (Weinig, p. 90). Williams's own early poetry (*The Silver Stair* [1912], *Divorce* [1920], *Windows of Night* [1924]) has strong affinities with Patmore.

22. *Athenaeum*, no. 1595 (1858); no. 1721 (1860); no. 1421 (1855).

23. *Critic* 21 (October 1860): 479, 506.

24. *The Angel in the House: The Betrothal* (London, 1854), p. 31.

25. In a letter of 1 March 1932 to his brother, A. E. Housman wrote: "Your generous offer to pass on Coventry Patmore [the article on Patmore for *Great Victorians*] to me has its allurements, for I have often idly thought of writing an essay on him and have been even inclined sometimes to regard it, as you say, in the light of a duty, because nobody admires his best poetry enough, though the stupid papists may fancy they do. But it would give me more trouble than you can imagine. . . . I should say as little as possible about his nasty mixture of piety and concupiscence; but his essay on English metre is the best thing ever written on the subject, though spoilt by one great mistake. . . ." (The letter unfortunately breaks off without disclosing the mistake!) (See Laurence Housman, *My Brother, A. E. Housman: Personal Recollections* . . . (New York, 1938), p. 183.

26. *Mystical Poems of Nuptial Love* (Boston, 1938), p. 129.

27. See J. C. Reid on the subject of Marie Lataste, *Mind and Art*, pp. 103ff.

Chapter Five

1. *Mind and Art*, pp. 281, 307.

2. Patmore's note to the 1863 edition (London), 2:234. See also Page, *Patmore: a Study in Poetry*, chap. 7.

3. This book is the beginning of the last harvest, which includes *The Unknown Eros*, odes 1–46, still in 1878—in the preceding year Patmore had published only twenty-one odes under this title—and in the following year the collective edition of *Poems by Coventry Patmore*, the poet's own choice of what was to survive and in what form. There was no other "complete" edition until after Patmore's death.

4. Page in a letter of 18 December 1935 to Derek Patmore enumerating their "points of difference" cites Derek's "blunder (which I wasn't alert enough to detect in the proofs: I am to blame) in *identifying* the fictitious wife in the *Departure* with her prototype Emily Patmore" (Princeton University Library Patmore collection).

5. *Mystical Poems of Nuptial Love*, p. 191.

6. *Pall Mall Gazette*, 7 November 1876.

7. Champneys, 2:118.

8. *A Daughter of Coventry Patmore*, p. 140.

9. *Reason and Beauty in the Poetic Mind* (Oxford, 1933), p. 177.

10. *Daughter*, p. 144.

11. The 1877 and 1878 editions have "attar," and *The Rod, the Root, and the Flower* (1895), p. 104, quotes it so. The 1906 and the Oxford *Poems* have "atta." The word "cloister'd," not in 1877 or 1878, appears in 1906 and Oxford to describe the "soul select" in the next sentence.

12. See M. Marie Thérèse Bisgood, *Cornelia Connelly: a Study in Fidelity* Westminster, Md., 1963).

13. See Patmore's handwritten note on the proof sheets of the *Unknown Eros*, British Library Ms. 41737, f. 50 verso.

14. Champneys, 1:261.

15. Terence Connelly's method in the commentary half of *Mystical Poems of Nuptial Love* is exhaustive annotation, with publication data, variants, and analogues. This book is particularly serviceable in lining up parallels with Patmore's prose, but Patmore himself would find that it makes an unnecessarily strong case for his dependence on strictly Roman Catholic sources. The critical reader might welcome a new book-length analysis of the major work of the last half of Patmore's career.

Chapter Six

1. Champneys, 1:154. See also Champneys, 1:117, for Patmore's avoidance of "direct portraiture as well in personality as in circumstances."

2. If "red" *is* red and not an abbreviation, a passage a little further on in the same article, marked with two ticks in the margin, "The heavenly

proprium, as to the good of love and the truth of faith respectively, denoted by red and white," might have suggested to Patmore the ladies initialed earlier.

3. In Boston College Library, Patmore Collection. The adjacent text reads: "There are two kinds of religious worship derived from the proprium: one in which the love of self and the world is all, denoted by Babel; the other in which the lumen of the natural man, and own intelligence is all, denoted by idols and strange gods, ill. and sh. 8941. No other is to be worshipped but the Lord, because he who worships the Lord is in humiliation, and in this state of humility there is a receding of the proprium . . ." (*Index*, p. 939). The last sentence is underlined by Patmore who calls this article on the "proprium" (in another marginal note near the beginning, p. 935) "a profound and thorough exposition of the doctrine of 'nature' and 'grace'" The note is signed "C. P. April 1863." Although there is no doubt about Patmore's theological interests before his reception into the Roman Catholic Church in 1864, the 1865 publication date of this edition of the *Arcana* index suggests that the observation above and possibly many others are recorded after the fact. For example, beside "Freedom from the proprium is nothing but evil, consisting in pleasures of all kinds and in contempt and hatred of others" (p. 939), Patmore writes: "'Good Society' in 1863." His acquaintance with the writings of Swedenborg probably began in the mid-1850s, but then and later he seems to have read chiefly for corroboration of what he already thought. His statement to Sutton, who was soon a more complete Swedenborgian than Patmore ever came near to being, of moral intention in *Tamerton Church-Tower* in 1853 could have found echoes in many spiritual or ethical writers, but Patmore tended to light upon less conventional sources with particular satisfaction.

4. See above, chapter 1, n. 65. It was young Emily who called Harriet "Honoria."

5. Champneys, 1:33, 72, 144, 346.

6. *Mind and Art of Coventry Patmore*, p. 32.

7. 1:250–62; 2:79–89.

8. Weinig, pp. 58ff.

9. Viola Meynell, *Alice Meynell: a Memoir* (London, 1929), p. 111.

10. Ibid., p. 114.

11. Ibid., pp. 99, 100.

12. Ibid., p. 100.

13. Reminiscences of Olivia Meynell Sowerby and her sister Madeleine on the occasion of the author's visit to the old Meynell home in Greatham, Sussex (summer 1965). It is to Mrs. Sowerby's prudent disposition of valuable material which Coventry Patmore gave to Alice Meynell that the manuscript of the *Unknown Eros* is in the British Library and many letters in the Patmore and Meynell collections at Boston College.

14. *Alice Meynell*, p. 101.

15. Ibid., p. 119.

16. Ibid., p. 122.

17. *The Rod, the Root, and the Flower*, p. 73–74.

18. Champneys, 1:134.

19. As for the shy and sickly Henry, who, when going up at eighteen for his university entrance examination, expostulated: "I know, dear Weenie, that this plan is the result of careful and kind thought, and I am afraid it will hurt you to hear I don't like it. . . . I am ashamed to be taken up to London and looked after . . ." (Champneys, 1:311).

20. Louise Wheaton, "Psyche and the Prophet," *Catholic World* 118 (1923): 355.

21. Champneys, 2:40–56.

22. *Mind and Art of Coventry Patmore*, p. 27.

23. Ibid., p. 28.

24. *Patmore: a Study in Poetry*, pp. 109–10.

25. *Mind and Art*, p. 271.

26. Ibid., p. 282.

Chapter Seven

1. *Courage in Politics*, p. 159.

2. *Mind and Art of Coventry Patmore*, p. 271.

3. Roth, ed., *English Metrical Law*, pp. 27–28.

4. Letter in Boston College Library, Patmore collection.

5. 27 (1857): 127–61.

6. *Courage in Politics*, p. 161.

7. *History of English Prosody* (London, 1923), p. 439.

8. Margaret R. Stobie, "Patmore's Theory and Hopkins' Practice," reprint from *University of Toronto Quarterly* 19 (1949): 65. See also W. H. Gardner. *Gerard Manley Hopkins* (New Haven, 1949), pp. 158ff.

9. Harold Whitehall, "Sprung Rhythm," in Kenyon Critics, *Gerard Manley Hopkins* (Norfolk, Conn., 1945), p. 176.

10. *Further Letters*, pp. 324–35.

11. Postscript of 16 October 1879, in *Letters of Gerard Manley Hopkins*, ed. Claude Colleer Abbott (London, 1935), p. 93.

12. *Further Letters*, p. 385. See also Patmore's side, pp. 361, 385, 390.

13. Ibid., p. 352.

14. Champneys, 2:248–49.

15. Undated, unpublished letter of Sidney Colvin to Coventry Patmore, probably 1886, in University of Nottingham Library, Patmore Collection, no. 1445.

16. Roth, p. 5.

17. *An Essay towards establishing the melody and measure of speech to be expressed and perpetuated by peculiar symbols* (London, 1775), p. viii.

18. *Prosodia Rationalis: or* [title as in preceding note], 2d ed. (1779), p. 163.

19. Roth, p. 15.

20. Ibid., p. 10.

21. *Further Letters*, p. 328.

22. Roth, p. 14.

23. Sister Marcella Marie Holloway, *Prosodic Theory of Gerard Manley Hopkins* (Washington, D.C., 1947), p. 94. Even Roth considers that Patmore "does not explicitly differentiate two distinct kinds of stress—the (lexical) 'accent' on a syllable and the (rhetorical) 'emphasis' on a word" (commentary in her critical edition of Patmore's essay), p. 64.

24. Roth, p. 15. The italics here and in subsequent quotations are Patmore's.

25. Ibid., p. 21. (A crotchet is a quarter note, a quaver an eighth.) A rare reference to Patmore as himself a musician occurs in J. Deighton Patmore, "Some Childish Recollections of Coventry Patmore," *Bookman* 82 (1932): 58, where the grandson repeats an anecdote of his father, Tennyson Patmore, who one day heard someone playing Chopin and to his surprise discovered it was Coventry—he had not known his father played the piano.

26. Roth, p. 9.

27. Ibid., p. 26.

28. Ibid., p. 39.

29. *Idea of Coventry Patmore*, p. 119. Patmore himself asserts "that the most inflexible, and as they are commonly thought, difficult metres, are the easiest for a novice to write decently in. The greater the frequency of the rhyme, and the more fixed the place of the grammatical pause, and the less liberty of changing the fundamental foot, the less will be the poet's obligation to originate his own rhythms" (Roth, pp. 48–49).

30. Roth, p. 41.

31. Ibid., p. 44.

32. Ibid., p. 48.

33. Ibid., p. 47.

34. Ibid., p. 9.

35. Letter to Owen Barfield, 10 June 1930, in *Letters of C. S. Lewis*, ed. W. H. Lewis (London, 1966), p. 141.

36. Roth, p. 16.

37. Frank Kermode, *The Sense of an Ending* (New York, 1967), p. 45.

38. Hereafter cited as *PA*.

39. Hereafter cited as *CP*.

40. Hereafter cited as *RP*.

Chapter Eight

1. *Positions et Propositions* (Paris: Gallimard, 1934), 2:29.

2. Translator (by 1906) of the *Dialogue of St. Catherine of Siena* and other mystical writings, student of the religious philosophy of Baron von Hügel, and eventually, as editor of the *Dublin Review*, in touch with the Meynell circle.

3. (Paris, 1957), pp. 307–18. See Valéry Larbaud's careful essay on these translations in *Ce Vice Impuni*, pp. 115–70. See also Alexandre Maurocordato, *Anglo-American Influence in Paul Claudel*, (part 1) *Coventry Patmore* (Geneva, 1964), pp. 148–58, and Marius-François Guyard, "De Patmore à Claudel," *Revue de Littérature Comparée* 33 (1959): 500–517.

4. Charles Du Bos, *Journal* 7 (July 1931–October 1932) (Paris, 1957), p. 229.

5. *What is Literature?* (New York, 1940), p. 83.

6. (Paris, 1906).

7. *Religio Poetae*. Page 5 of the 1907 edition has "All realities will sing, but nothing else will."

8. Brémond, *Prayer and Poetry*, trans. Algar Thorold (London, 1927), p. 138.

9. *Religio Poetae*, pp. 2–3. (Thorold's otherwise reliable translation seems to have Englished Brémond's French translation of Patmore instead of quoting its source.) See also Patmore's essay, "Real Apprehension," *Religio Poetae*, pp. 77–84.

10. *Month* 96 (July–December 1900), 561–73, reprinted as "Poet and Mystic" in *The Faith of the Millions* (London, 1901). This was a review-article on Champneys's *Memoirs and Correspondence of Coventry Patmore*.

11. 1952–1955, trans. by Frances Forrest (Baltimore, 1963), pp. 283–84.

12. *Images de la Vierge* (Paris, 1963), p. 18.

13. *Seven Unpublished Poems by Coventry Patmore to Alice Meynell*, privately printed by Francis Meynell (London, 1922).

14. Retained in the preface to the 1906 *Poems of Coventry Patmore*, ed. Basil Champneys, p. v.

Selected Bibliography

Only the principal printed editions and collections of Patmore's verse and prose are given in the primary section here. (For unpublished letters and other manuscript sources see acknowledgments.) J. C. Reid's 1957 bibliography in *Mind and Art of Coventry Patmore* is the most detailed we have, adding to Frederick Page's list of Patmore's contributions to periodicals, and including a fairly exhaustive list of articles about Patmore. A few of Reid's attributions are corrected by Alfred Thomas in "The Literary Criticism of Coventry Patmore: an exposition and commentary with special reference to his reviews of contemporary poets" (M.A. thesis, University of London, 1960), and by Walter Houghton and the other editors of the *Wellesley Index to Victorian Periodicals, 1824–1900* (Toronto, 1966–).

The notes to the present study refer to several items of Patmore's unreprinted prose; these entries are not repeated in the bibliography. Likewise many more secondary sources are cited in the notes than appear in the bibliography, which is limited to works dealing mainly with Patmore and his closest associates, excluding innumerable works where mention is made of Patmore in connection with their chief subjects, e.g., his father's circle, the Pre-Raphaelites, or Gerard Manley Hopkins.

PRIMARY SOURCES

Poems. London: Moxon, 1844. Patmore's first book, immature but significant, published at his father's insistence.

Tamerton Church-Tower and Other Poems. London: Pickering, 1853. This includes revised versions of most of the 1844 poems as well as new material.

The Angel in the House: The Betrothal. London: Parker, 1854. The author's name does not appear on the title page. This is the only edition bearing the following dedication: "The Writer of this poem inscribes it: To His Daughter Emily."

The Angel in the House: Book II, The Espousals. London: Parker, 1856. The author's name is still withheld.

The Angel in the House: Book I, The Betrothal; Book II, The Espousals. 2d ed. London: Parker, 1858. Patmore's name is given. The third edition in 1860 has similar title page.

Faithful For Ever. London: Parker, 1860. This is the third book of the *Angel* but does not so indicate on the title page.

The Victories of Love. London: Macmillan, 1863. The fourth and final book of the *Angel.* An American edition is recorded (Boston: Burnham, 1862). Ticknor and Fields (Boston) had published separate editions of the *Betrothal, Espousals,* and *Faithful For Ever* between 1855 and 1861. American editions continue to appear into the 1870s, but only of the parts of the *Angel,* and of the *Children's Garland,* an anthology edited by Patmore.

The Children's Garland. London: Macmillan, 1862. This very popular anthology went into several editions. Patmore's wife collaborated in the selection of poems.

The Angel in the House. 2 vols. London: Macmillan, 1863. This is the first edition of the whole four-part poem, and the first with the dedication: "To the memory of her by whom and for whom I became a poet."

Odes. Privately printed, 1868. Terence Connolly issued in 1936 a facsimile reproduction of this rare edition of nine odes, "primarily intended for students of Patmore at Boston College Graduate School."

Bryan Waller Procter (Barry Cornwall). An autobiographical fragment and biographical notes. London: Bell, 1877. Edited by Coventry Patmore at the request of Mrs. Procter.

The Unknown Eros and Other Odes I–XXXI. London: Bell, 1877.

The Unknown Eros . . . I–XLVI. London: Bell, 1878. The fuller edition contained the original nine odes, several others which had appeared only under the initials "C.P." and a few which were later moved out of the *Eros* sequence but retained in another section of the final collected poems.

Amelia. Privately printed. 1878.

Amelia, Tamerton Church-Tower, etc., with a Prefatory Study of English Metrical Law. London: Bell, 1878. The essay on "English Metrical Critics" had appeared in the *North British Review* in 1857.

Poems. 4 vols. London: Bell, 1879. Consists of the *Amelia* volume containing also all the early poems (1844–1853) which Patmore wanted to preserve, a two-book *Angel in the House,* a two-book *Victories of Love,* and a 42-ode *Unknown Eros.*

Florilegium Amantis. Edited by Richard Garnett. London: Bell, 1879. A selection of Patmore's poems.

St. Bernard on the Love of God. Translated by Marianne Caroline and Coventry Patmore. London: Kegan Paul, 1881. Patmore finished this after his second wife's death.

Poems. 2 vols. London: Bell, 1886. Includes poems by Henry Patmore. Many times reprinted, this was the "final" edition as Patmore saw it through the press.

How I Managed and Improved My Estate. London: Bell, 1886. Account of Heron's Ghyll, originally brief essays in the *St. James Gazette.*

Hastings, Lewes, Rye, and the Sussex Marshes. London: Bell, 1887. Another series of *St. James's* articles.

Principle in Art. London: Bell, 1889. A collection of Patmore's later essays, arranged by himself. Several subsequent editions.

Religio Poetae. London: Bell, 1893. Another collection of essays. Later editions include one with *Principle in Art* in a single volume (London: Duckworth, 1913).

The Rod, the Root and the Flower. London: Bell, 1895. Aphorisms composed over a lifetime, probably embodying much of the mystical writing that would have gone into *Sponsa Dei.* Posthumous editions add more extracts gleaned from unpublished notes and from the original manuscript, notably Derek Patmore's (edited with an introduction, London: Grey Walls Press, 1950).

The Poetry of Pathos and Delight. Selected by Alice Meynell. London: Heinemann, 1896.

Poems. Edited with an introduction by Basil Champneys. London: Bell, 1906. One-volume edition following the 1886 text but omitting Henry Patmore's poems.

Courage in Politics and Other Essays, 1885–1896. Edited by Frederick Page. London: Oxford University Press, 1921. Thirty-nine essays not otherwise reprinted. An appendix contains the basic bibliography of Patmore's periodical contributions.

Seven Unpublished Poems by Coventry Patmore to Alice Meynell. Privately printed by Francis Meynell, 1922.

Mystical Poems of Nuptial Love. Edited with notes by Terence Connolly, S.J. Boston: Bruce Humphries, 1938. The *Wedding Sermon* and the odes, with variant readings, data on first publication, commentary in the light of probable sources.

Poems. Edited with an introduction by Frederick Page. London: Oxford University Press, 1949. The standard edition, following the 1886 text but in chronological order of book publication.

Further Letters of Gerard Manley Hopkins, including his correspondence with Coventry Patmore. Edited by Claude Colleer Abbott. 2d ed. London: Oxford University Press, 1956.

"Essay on English Metrical Law": a Critical Edition with a Commentary. Edited by Sister Mary Augustine Roth, R.S.M. Washington, D.C.: Catholic University of America Press, 1961. Doctoral dissertation.

SECONDARY SOURCES

BURDETT, OSBERT. *The Idea of Coventry Patmore.* London: Humphrey Milford, 1921. Remains valuable for analysis of the *Angel* and for presentation of Patmore as philosopher of love.

CHAMPNEYS, BASIL. *Memoirs and Correspondence of Coventry Patmore.* 2 vols. London: Bell, 1900. Official biography, prepared by a personal friend assisted by the poet's widow.

GOSSE, EDMUND. *Coventry Patmore.* New York: Scribner, 1905. Earliest book-length critical study; firsthand, anecdotal account.

GUYARD, MARIUS-FRANÇOIS. "De Patmore à Claudel." *Revue de la Littérature Comparée* 33 (1959): 500–517. Discusses Claudel's interest in and translations of Patmore's odes.

HOLLOWAY, JOHN. "Patmore, Donne, and the 'Wit of Love'." In *The Charted Mirror.* New York: Horizon Press, 1962. Examines Patmore's interest in and affinities with Donne.

HOLLOWAY, SISTER MARCELLA MARIE. *Prosodic Theory of Gerard Manley Hopkins.* Washington, D.C.: Catholic University of America Press, 1947. Doctoral dissertation; refers also to Patmore's prosody.

JOHNSON, LIONEL. "Coventry Patmore's Genius." In *Post Liminium: Essays and Critical Papers.* Edited by Thomas Whittemore. New York: Mitchell Kennerley, 1912. Originally a *Daily Chronicle* review (22 October 1900) of Champneys's *Memoirs;* a fulsome appreciation.

LARBAUD, VALÉRY. *Ce Vice Impuni.* Paris: Messein, 1925. Good on P. G. Patmore as well as on Coventry's reputation in France.

McELRATH, JOSEPH R. "Coventry Patmore's 'The Angel in the House': The Experience of Divine Love." *Cithara* 10 (1970): 45–53. A recent look at Patmore's "middle ground between sensualism and intellectualism."

MAUROCORDATO, ALEXANDRE. *Anglo-American Influences in Paul Claudel.* (1) *Coventry Patmore.* Geneva: Droz, 1964. Explores common themes.

MEYNELL, VIOLA. *Alice Meynell: a Memoir.* London: Burns, Oates and Washbourne, 1929. Contains a useful chapter on Patmore's friendship with the Meynells.

———. *Francis Thompson and Wilfrid Meynell: a Memoir.* London: Hollis and Carter, 1952. Deals with Patmore's friendship with Thompson; several letters and an account of Patmore manuscripts in the Meynell library (Olivia Meynell Sowerby has since placed some of these in Boston College and other Patmore collections).

NICOLL, W. ROBERTSON, and WISE, THOMAS J. *Literary Anecdotes of the Nineteenth Century.* London: Hodder and Stoughton, 1896. Background on related figures; account of Emily Augusta Patmore.

OLIVER, EDWARD JAMES. *Coventry Patmore.* New York: Sheed and Ward, 1956. A short but insightful biography for the general reader; contains new material on Henry Patmore.

PAGE, FREDERICK. *Patmore: a Study in Poetry.* London: Oxford University Press, 1933. Still essential to a serious reading of Patmore; Page brought a lifetime's study of Patmore to his analysis.

PATMORE, DEREK. *Portrait of My Family.* London: Constable, 1935.

———. *Life and Times of Coventry Patmore.* London: Constable, 1949. Popular biographies by a great grandson of Coventry Patmore; not totally reliable.

PATMORE, GERTRUDE. *Our Pets and Playfellows in Air, Earth and Water.* Illustrated by Bertha Patmore. London: Bell, 1880. Glimpses of a Victorian household menagerie shed light on the Patmore legend.

PLATT, PHILIP WALLACE. "The Spiritual Vision of Coventry Patmore: a Study of his Religious Faith and its Expression in his Work." Ph.D. dissertation, University of Toronto, 1976. An important study of an aspect of Patmore not dealt with adequately elsewhere.

PRAZ, MARIO. *Hero in Eclipse in Victorian Fiction*. London: Oxford University Press, 1956. Appendix, "The Epic of the Everyday," discusses the *Angel in the House*.

REID, JOHN COWIE. *Mind and Art of Coventry Patmore*. London: Routledge and Kegan Paul, 1957. A basic modern study with the fullest Patmore bibliography yet published.

ROSSETTI, WILLIAM MICHAEL. *Praeraphaelite Diaries and Letters*. London: Hurst and Blackett, 1900. Glimpses of Coventry Patmore as the PRB saw him.

SHMIEFSKY, MARVEL. "'Principle in Art' as Criticism in the Mainstream." *Victorian Newsletter*, no. 26 (Fall 1964): 28–32. Recognizes the viability of much of Patmore's thought.

STOBIE, MARGARET R. "Patmore's Theory and Hopkins' Practice." *University of Toronto Quarterly* 19 (1949).

WEINIG, SISTER MARY ANTHONY. "Coventry Patmore in the Correspondence of his Contemporaries." M.A. thesis, Fordham University, 1951.

WHEATON, LOUISE et al. *A Daughter of Coventry Patmore, Sister Mary Christina, S.H.C.J.* London: Longmans, Green, 1924. Biography of Emily Honoria Patmore.

———. "Emily Honoria Patmore." *Dublin Review* 163 (1918): 207–33. Mother St. Ignatius Wheaton contributed several articles to the *Dublin* under Wilfrid Meynell's editorship.

———. "Psyche and the Prophet." *Catholic World* 118 (1923): 355–66. Deals particularly with Emily Honoria Patmore's response to and probable influence on her father's religious poetry.

Index